THE NEW NOWZARADAN MEAL PLAN SYSTEM

1800 Days of Tailored Recipes Designed to Simplify Your Journey to Lasting Health and Effortless Weight Loss

Darla Robson

TABLE OF CONTENTS

CHAPTER 7: BREAKFAST RECIPES FOR ENERGY AND WEIGHT LOSS

CHAPTER 8: LUNCH RECIPES FOR A BALANCED MIDDAY MEAL

CHAPTER 9: DINNER RECIPES FOR A SATISFYING END TO YOUR DAY

CHAPTER 10: SNACK AND DESSERT RECIPES TO KEEP YOU ON TRACK

1.1 The Philosophy Behind the Plan

Dr. Nowzaradan's philosophy on weight loss and health begins with a fundamental understanding: weight loss is not just a goal but a process—a deeply personal journey that requires commitment, patience, and a willingness to change not only what we eat but how we think about food. His approach is rooted in decades of medical experience, where he has seen firsthand the struggles and triumphs of countless individuals battling obesity. What sets his philosophy apart is its holistic nature; it's not merely about reducing numbers on a scale but about fostering a sustainable, healthy lifestyle that can be maintained long after the weight is lost.

At the heart of Dr. Nowzaradan's approach is the concept of mindfulness. In today's fast-paced world, it's easy to eat on autopilot—grabbing whatever is convenient, often without considering the nutritional value or even the hunger cues our bodies send us. Dr. Nowzaradan encourages a return to intentional eating, where every food choice is made with awareness and purpose. This doesn't mean eating becomes an obsession, but rather a conscious act that aligns with our health goals. When you start to pay attention to what you're eating and why you're eating it, you begin

to see food not just as fuel, but as a tool for achieving better health.

Another key element of his philosophy is the emphasis on simplicity. The diet and wellness industry are saturated with complex diets that often require special ingredients, supplements, or elaborate preparation methods. Dr. Nowzaradan's plan, in contrast, is refreshingly straightforward. It's built around the idea that the best foods are those that are closest to their natural state—whole foods that are minimally processed and rich in essential nutrients. By focusing on simple, nutritious foods, the plan not only makes weight loss achievable but also sustainable. The simplicity of the plan is what makes it adaptable to real life, where time and resources may be limited.

This simplicity also extends to the structure of meals. Instead of advocating for strict calorie counting or complicated meal plans, Dr. Nowzaradan promotes the idea of balance. A balanced meal includes the right proportions of proteins, carbohydrates, and fats, each playing a critical role in your body's functioning. Proteins help build and repair tissues, carbohydrates provide energy, and fats support cell function and hormone production. Understanding this balance is crucial because it shifts the focus from deprivation to nourishment. You're not just cutting calories; you're providing your body with what it needs to thrive.

But what truly distinguishes Dr. Nowzaradan's approach is its flexibility. He recognizes that no two bodies are the same, and as such, no single diet plan will work for everyone. His method is not about one-size-fits-all solutions but about personalization. The plan is designed to be tailored to the individual's specific needs, taking into account their lifestyle, preferences, and any underlying health conditions.

This personalized approach is critical for long-term success because it allows individuals to find a way of eating that they can stick with, not just for a few weeks or months, but for life.

Education is another cornerstone of Dr. Nowzaradan's philosophy. He believes that for individuals to make lasting changes, they need to understand the principles behind the plan. This means educating them about nutrition, how different foods affect the body, and the importance of portion control. When you know why certain foods are better for you and how they impact your health, it becomes easier to make choices that align with your goals. Education empowers individuals to take control of their health, giving them the tools they need to succeed not just during the weight loss phase but throughout their lives.

Dr. Nowzaradan also emphasizes the importance of setting realistic, achievable goals. Many people start their weight loss journey with lofty ambitions, hoping to shed large amounts of weight in a short period. While it's good to be ambitious, it's also important to be realistic. Dr. Nowzaradan advocates for setting smaller, incremental goals that are more attainable. This approach not only makes the process less overwhelming but also helps build momentum. As you achieve these smaller goals, you gain confidence and motivation to keep going. It's a marathon, not a sprint, and each step forward is progress.

Central to this philosophy is the idea of accountability. Dr. Nowzaradan teaches that while external support from friends, family, or a healthcare provider is valuable, the most important aspect of success is personal responsibility. This means being honest with yourself about your habits, tracking your progress, and staying committed to the plan even when it gets challenging. Accountability is about recognizing that you have the power to change your life. It's not about blame but about empowerment. When you take ownership of your health journey, you're more likely to stick with it, even when the going gets tough.

Compassion is another vital component of Dr. Nowzaradan's philosophy. He understands that weight loss is not just a physical challenge but an emotional one as well. Many people struggle with emotional eating, using food as a way to cope with stress, sadness, or boredom. Dr. Nowzaradan approaches these issues with empathy, recognizing that everyone has different triggers and challenges. His plan includes strategies for dealing with these emotional aspects of eating, helping individuals develop healthier ways to cope with their feelings. This compassionate approach helps create a supportive environment where individuals feel encouraged rather than judged.

Patience is perhaps one of the most difficult aspects of weight loss, yet it's one of the most crucial. In a world that often prizes quick results, Dr. Nowzaradan reminds us that real, lasting change takes time. The body needs time to adjust to new habits, and the mind needs time to adapt to a new way of thinking about food and health. Dr. Nowzaradan encourages his patients to be patient with themselves, to celebrate small victories, and to view setbacks not as failures but as learning opportunities. Patience is about recognizing that the journey to better health is ongoing, and that progress, no matter how slow, is still progress.

In essence, Dr. Nowzaradan's philosophy on weight loss and health is about creating a balanced, sustainable lifestyle that prioritizes long-term well-being over short-term results. It's about understanding that true health comes from nourishing the body, mind, and spirit. It's about embracing simplicity, practicing mindfulness, and cultivating patience. Most importantly, it's about taking control of your health journey with the knowledge, tools, and support you need to succeed. This philosophy is not just a diet; it's a way of life—a path to lasting health and happiness.

1.2 THE SCIENCE OF NUTRITION AND WEIGHT LOSS:

The science of nutrition and weight loss is a complex, yet fascinating, field that underpins the effectiveness of Dr. Nowzaradan's meal plan. Understanding these principles is essential to appreciate why certain foods are included in the plan, why others are minimized, and how this knowledge can empower you to achieve your health goals.

The Principle of Energy Balance

At the foundation of weight loss is the concept of energy balance, which is essentially the relationship between the calories you consume and the calories your body expends. This balance determines whether you gain, lose, or maintain weight. When you consume more calories than your body uses for energy, the excess is stored as fat, leading to weight gain. Conversely, when you consume fewer calories than your body needs, it begins to burn stored fat for energy, resulting in weight loss.

Dr. Nowzaradan's meal plan is designed to create a calorie deficit—where the energy intake from food is less than the energy expenditure—while still providing the necessary nutrients to maintain health. This is achieved not by extreme calorie restriction, which can be unsustainable and unhealthy, but by promoting a balanced, nutrient-dense diet that supports your body's needs while facilitating gradual, sustainable weight loss.

The Role of Macronutrients

Macronutrients—proteins, carbohydrates, and fats—are the primary components of our diet and each plays a vital role in health and weight management. Understanding how these macronutrients interact with your body is key to making informed food choices.

Proteins are crucial for the repair and growth of tissues, including muscle. They have a high thermic effect, meaning the body uses more energy to digest and metabolize them compared to fats and carbohydrates. This not only boosts metabolism slightly but also increases satiety, helping you feel full longer and reducing the likelihood of overeating. Dr. Nowzaradan's plan emphasizes lean protein sources, such as poultry, fish, and legumes, to support muscle maintenance during weight loss while minimizing unnecessary fat intake.

Carbohydrates are the body's primary source of energy, particularly for the brain and muscles. However, not all carbohydrates are created equal. Simple carbohydrates, like those found in sugary snacks and refined grains, cause rapid spikes in blood sugar, followed by crashes that can lead to hunger and overeating. On the other hand, complex carbohydrates, such as those found in whole grains, vegetables, and legumes, are digested more slowly, providing sustained energy and helping to maintain stable blood sugar levels. Dr. Nowzaradan's plan focuses on these complex carbohydrates, ensuring that your body receives the energy it needs without the negative effects of sugar spikes and crashes.

Fats are often misunderstood in the context of weight loss. While fats are calorie-dense, they are also essential for various bodily functions, including hormone production and nutrient absorption. The key is to choose the right types of fats. Unsaturated fats, found in foods like avocados, nuts, and olive oil, are heart-healthy and should be included in moderation. Saturated fats, which are found in animal products like butter and red meat, should be limited, while trans fats, found in many processed foods, should be avoided altogether. Dr. Nowzaradan's plan includes healthy fats in controlled portions to support overall health without contributing to weight gain.

Micronutrients: The Unsung Heroes

While macronutrients get most of the attention, micronutrients—vitamins and minerals—are just as important. They are involved in virtually every process in the body, from energy production to immune function. For example, calcium is essential for bone health, iron is crucial for transporting oxygen in the blood, and vitamin C supports the immune system.

Dr. Nowzaradan's meal plan is rich in fruits, vegetables, and whole foods, ensuring that you receive a broad spectrum of these essential micronutrients. By focusing on nutrient-dense foods, the plan helps you meet your nutritional needs without excessive calorie intake, supporting both weight loss and overall health.

Portion Control: The Key to Sustainable Eating

Portion sizes have grown dramatically over the years, contributing to the rise in obesity. Dr. Nowzaradan's approach to nutrition places a strong emphasis on portion control. Rather than eliminating entire food groups or severely restricting calories, the plan encourages moderate portions of a variety of foods.

Learning to recognize appropriate portion sizes is crucial. It's not just about eating less but about eating in a way that satisfies your hunger and meets your nutritional needs without excess. This balanced approach helps prevent the feelings of deprivation that often lead to overeating or giving up on a diet altogether.

Hydration and Its Role in Weight Loss

Hydration is a critical yet often overlooked component of nutrition and weight loss. Water plays a key role in digestion, nutrient absorption, and the elimination of waste products from the body. It also helps regulate body temperature and lubricates joints, making it essential for overall health.

Moreover, drinking water before meals can help control appetite, as thirst is sometimes mistaken for hunger. Staying hydrated throughout the day ensures that your body functions optimally and supports your weight loss efforts by helping you feel fuller, more energized, and less likely to overeat.

The Timing of Meals: Consistency is Key

The timing of your meals can have a significant impact on your weight loss success. Regular meal times help regulate your metabolism and prevent extreme hunger, which can lead to overeating. Skipping meals, especially breakfast, can slow down your metabolism and increase the likelihood of making poor food choices later in the day.

Dr. Nowzaradan's plan encourages eating smaller, balanced meals at regular intervals. This approach helps maintain stable blood sugar levels, supports steady energy throughout the day, and prevents the extreme hunger that often leads to overeating or choosing unhealthy foods.

The Psychological Component: Mindful Eating

Mindful eating is an essential part of Dr. Nowzaradan's nutritional philosophy. It's not just about what you eat but also about how you eat. Mindful eating involves paying full attention to the experience of eating and drinking, both inside and outside the body. It's about being aware of the colors, smells, textures, and flavors of your food, as well as your body's hunger and fullness cues.

By practicing mindful eating, you can develop a healthier relationship with food, reduce overeating, and enjoy your meals more. It also helps you recognize emotional triggers that might lead to eating when you're not truly hungry, allowing you to address these issues in healthier ways.

The science of nutrition and weight loss, as integrated into Dr. Nowzaradan's meal plan, is about more than just reducing calories. It's about understanding how different nutrients work together to support your health, learning to manage portion sizes, staying hydrated, and being mindful of when and how you eat. By embracing these principles, you can create a balanced and sustainable approach to weight loss that not only helps you shed pounds but also improves your overall well-being.

1.3 SETTING REALISTIC AND ACHIEVABLE GOALS

Setting realistic and achievable goals is one of the most crucial steps in any successful weight loss journey. It's the foundation upon which all other efforts are built. When goals are clear, specific, and attainable, they provide direction and motivation, transforming a vague desire for better health into a concrete plan of action. Dr. Nowzaradan's approach to goal-setting is both practical and empowering, encouraging individuals to create goals that are tailored to their unique circumstances and capable of sustaining long-term success.

Understanding the Importance of Realistic Goals

The temptation to aim for drastic, rapid weight loss is strong, especially in a culture that glorifies quick fixes and overnight transformations. However, Dr. Nowzaradan's experience has shown that setting overly ambitious goals can be counterproductive. When goals are too extreme, they often lead to frustration, burnout, and eventually, abandonment of the plan altogether. Realistic goals, on the other hand, are achievable, sustainable, and foster a sense of accomplishment that builds momentum over time.

Realistic goals are grounded in a deep understanding of your current health, lifestyle, and limitations. They take into account your starting point—whether you're beginning your journey with a significant amount of weight to lose, or you're looking to shed just a few pounds. Dr. Nowzaradan emphasizes the importance of setting goals that are challenging enough to drive change but not so daunting that they feel unattainable.

The SMART Goal Framework

One of the most effective ways to set realistic and achievable goals is by using the SMART framework. SMART stands for Specific, Measurable, Achievable, Relevant, and Time-bound. This method helps break down your larger aspirations into manageable steps, each with a clear objective and timeline.

Specific: A goal needs to be clear and specific. Instead of saying, "I want to lose weight," a more specific goal would be, "I want to lose 10 pounds in the next three months." This specificity helps you focus your efforts and understand exactly what you're working towards.

Measurable: Goals should be measurable so you can track your progress. This might involve regular weigh-ins, keeping a food diary, or monitoring your physical activity. Having measurable outcomes allows you to see how far you've come and adjust your efforts if necessary.

Achievable: While it's important to set goals that challenge you, they must also be realistic. Losing 50 pounds in a month is not achievable or healthy, but aiming to lose 1-2 pounds per week is both realistic and sustainable.

Relevant: Your goals should align with your overall health objectives and personal circumstances. If your primary aim is to improve your cardiovascular health, setting a goal to increase your daily steps or engage in regular aerobic exercise would be more relevant than focusing solely on weight loss.

Time-bound: Every goal needs a deadline. Having a time frame creates a sense of urgency and helps keep you accountable. Whether your goal is short-term, like drinking more water every day for a week, or long-term, like reaching your target weight by the end of the year, setting a deadline keeps you on track.

Personalizing Your Goals

No two people are alike, and therefore, no two weight loss journeys are the same. Dr. Nowzaradan's approach to goal-setting is deeply personal, encouraging individuals to tailor their goals to fit their unique lives. Personalization is key to creating goals that are not only realistic but also meaningful.

Start by reflecting on your motivations for losing weight. Are you looking to improve your health, boost your energy levels, or enhance your quality of life? Understanding your "why" is essential for setting goals that resonate with you on a deeper level. When your goals are aligned with your personal values and desires, they become more than just numbers on a scale—they become steps toward a better, healthier you.

Consider your lifestyle when setting goals. If you have a busy schedule, it might not be realistic to commit to an hour of exercise every day. Instead, you could start with a goal of incorporating 15-20 minutes of physical activity into your day, whether that's a morning walk, a quick home workout, or even taking the stairs instead of the elevator. The key is to create goals that fit seamlessly into your daily routine, making them easier to stick to.

It's also important to consider any barriers you might face. If you struggle with emotional eating, for instance, setting a goal to manage stress through healthier outlets like meditation or journaling can be just as important as setting a weight loss goal. By acknowledging and addressing these challenges upfront, you create a more realistic plan that anticipates obstacles and includes strategies for overcoming them.

Celebrating Small Victories

As you progress on your weight loss journey, it's important to celebrate the small victories along the way. Dr. Nowzaradan encourages his patients to acknowledge every achievement, no matter how small, because each step forward is a sign of progress. Whether it's losing your first five pounds, resisting the temptation to overeat, or completing a week of consistent exercise, these milestones deserve recognition.

Celebrating small victories helps build confidence and keeps you motivated to continue. It shifts the focus from what you haven't yet achieved to what you've already accomplished, reinforcing the positive behaviors that contribute to long-term success. Over time, these small victories add up, leading to significant changes in your health and well-being.

Adjusting Goals as You Progress

Flexibility is an essential aspect of setting realistic goals. As you progress, you may find that your initial goals need to be adjusted. Perhaps you're losing weight faster than anticipated, or maybe you've encountered challenges that require a change in approach. Dr. Nowzaradan's philosophy encourages regular reassessment of your goals to ensure they remain relevant and achievable.

Adjusting your goals is not a sign of failure; it's a reflection of your evolving journey. It's important to remain adaptable, recognizing that the path to better health is rarely a straight line. By staying flexible and open to change, you can continue to set goals that are realistic, achievable, and aligned with your long-term vision for health and wellness.

The Power of Accountability

Accountability plays a critical role in achieving your goals. Dr. Nowzaradan emphasizes the importance of holding yourself accountable, whether through self-monitoring, regular check-ins with a healthcare provider, or seeking support from friends and family. Accountability keeps you focused and committed, providing the structure and encouragement needed to stay on track.

Sharing your goals with others can also be a powerful motivator. When you involve others in your journey, you create a support system that can offer encouragement, advice, and even a little healthy competition. Whether it's a workout buddy, a family member, or an online community, having people who share your goals can make the process more enjoyable and less isolating.

Setting realistic and achievable goals is the cornerstone of successful weight loss and overall health improvement. Dr. Nowzaradan's approach is about more than just numbers on a scale—it's about creating a personalized, flexible plan that aligns with your unique life and motivations. By using the SMART framework, personalizing your goals, celebrating your progress, and holding yourself accountable, you can set the stage for long-term success.

2.1 MACRONUTRIENTS: PROTEINS, FATS, AND CARBOHYDRATES

When it comes to building a balanced plate, understanding the role of macronutrients—proteins, fats, and carbohydrates—is essential. These three components are the primary nutrients that make up the bulk of our diet, and each plays a crucial role in maintaining health and supporting your body's functions. Dr. Nowzaradan's meal plan emphasizes the importance of balancing these macronutrients to create a diet that not only promotes weight loss but also sustains energy, supports metabolism, and ensures overall well-being.

The Power of Protein

Protein is often referred to as the building block of life, and for good reason. Every cell in your body contains protein, making it vital for the growth, repair, and maintenance of tissues. From your muscles to your skin, and even your hair and nails, protein is at the core of it all. But beyond its structural role, protein is a key player in weight management and metabolic health.

When you eat protein, your body breaks it down into amino acids, which are then used to repair tissues, produce enzymes and hormones, and support immune function. This process requires energy, and protein has a higher thermic effect than carbohydrates

or fats, meaning your body uses more energy to digest and metabolize protein. This not only boosts your metabolism slightly but also contributes to a feeling of fullness and satisfaction after meals, which can help control appetite and prevent overeating.

Dr. Nowzaradan's meal plan encourages the inclusion of high-quality protein sources, such as lean meats, fish, eggs, legumes, and plant-based proteins like tofu and tempeh. The focus is on proteins that provide essential amino acids without excessive amounts of saturated fat or calories. By prioritizing protein at each meal, you not only support your body's repair and maintenance needs but also create a foundation for sustained energy and satiety throughout the day.

Moreover, protein is particularly important when you're losing weight. As you shed pounds, it's crucial to preserve lean muscle mass. Muscle tissue burns more calories at rest compared to fat tissue, so maintaining your muscle mass helps keep your metabolism active even as you lose weight. This is why protein is often considered a cornerstone of any effective weight loss plan.

The Truth About Fats

Fats have long been misunderstood in the context of diet and health. For years, they were demonized as the primary culprit behind weight gain and heart disease. However, the narrative around fats has evolved, and we now understand that not all fats are created equal. In fact, fats are essential to your diet, playing a critical role in hormone production, nutrient absorption, and overall cellular function.

Fats are the most energy-dense macronutrient, providing nine calories per gram—more than double the calories provided by proteins or carbohydrates. This makes fats an efficient source of energy, especially for long-duration activities and when carbohydrates are in short supply. However, the type of fat you consume is what really matters.

Unsaturated fats, which are found in foods like olive oil, avocados, nuts, and fatty fish, are known for their heart-healthy benefits. These fats help reduce inflammation, lower bad cholesterol levels, and are essential for brain health. Incorporating unsaturated fats into your diet can improve cardiovascular health while also providing the necessary building blocks for hormone production.

Saturated fats, on the other hand, should be consumed in moderation. These fats are typically found in animal products like red meat, butter, and full-fat dairy. While they're not inherently bad, excessive consumption of saturated fats has been linked to increased cholesterol levels and a higher risk of heart disease. Dr. Nowzaradan's meal plan advises limiting saturated fat intake by choosing leaner cuts of meat and opting for plant-based oils instead of butter or lard.

Then there are trans fats, which are artificially created through a process called hydrogenation and are commonly found in processed foods, baked goods, and margarine. These fats are the most harmful, associated with a significant increase in the risk of heart disease. Dr. Nowzaradan's plan strongly recommends avoiding trans fats altogether due to their negative health impacts.

By understanding the different types of fats and their roles in your body, you can make informed choices that support both weight loss and long-term health. Incorporating healthy fats in moderation helps you feel satisfied after meals, supports nutrient absorption, and provides the essential fatty acids your body needs for optimal functioning.

Carbohydrates: Fuel for the Body

Carbohydrates often get a bad reputation in diet circles, particularly in the context of weight loss. However, carbohydrates are your body's primary source of energy, especially for the brain and muscles. Understanding the difference between simple and complex carbohydrates is key to making smart choices that fuel your body without contributing to weight gain.

Simple carbohydrates, which include sugars and refined grains like white bread and pastries, are quickly broken down by the body and can cause rapid spikes in blood sugar. These spikes are often followed by crashes, leading to feelings of hunger and cravings for more sugary or starchy foods. This rollercoaster effect can contribute to overeating and weight gain, which is why Dr. Nowzaradan's plan advises minimizing simple carbohydrates.

Complex carbohydrates, on the other hand, are digested more slowly, providing a steady release of energy over time. These are found in whole grains, vegetables, legumes, and fruits. Complex carbs are not only a better source of sustained energy but also come packed with fiber, vitamins, and minerals that are essential for overall health. Fiber, in particular, plays a crucial role in digestion and helps keep you full longer, making it an important component of a weight management plan.

Dr. Nowzaradan's meal plan encourages the consumption of complex carbohydrates as part of a balanced diet. Whole grains like brown rice, quinoa, and oats, along with a variety of vegetables and legumes, should form the foundation of your carbohydrate intake. These foods provide the necessary energy to fuel your daily activities while also supporting digestive health and stabilizing blood sugar levels.

It's also important to note that not all carbohydrates are created equal, even within the categories of simple and complex. For instance, fruits contain natural sugars but also provide fiber and important nutrients, making them a better choice than refined sugar or sweets. Similarly, vegetables offer a wealth of vitamins, minerals, and fiber with relatively few calories, making them an ideal source of carbohydrates for weight loss and overall health.

Finding the Right Balance

The key to building a balanced plate lies in finding the right proportion of proteins, fats, and carbohydrates that works for your body and your goals. Dr. Nowzaradan's approach is not about extreme restriction or eliminating entire food groups, but rather about creating a harmonious balance that provides all the nutrients your body needs.

Each macronutrient plays a unique role in your diet, and understanding these roles helps you make informed choices that support your health and weight loss efforts. By incorporating a variety of nutrient-dense foods from each macronutrient category, you can create meals that are satisfying, nourishing, and aligned with your goals.

Remember, balance is not just about what you eat but also how you eat. Mindful eating practices, such as paying attention to hunger and fullness cues and savoring each bite, can enhance your relationship with food and help you maintain a healthy diet in the long term. Dr. Nowzaradan's meal plan is designed to be flexible, allowing you to adjust your macronutrient intake based on your individual needs, preferences, and progress.

In the end, understanding the role of macronutrients in your diet is about more than just counting calories or grams of protein. It's about recognizing how each nutrient contributes to your overall health and well-being, and making choices that nourish your body, fuel your life, and support your journey toward a healthier you. By embracing a balanced approach to eating, you can achieve your weight loss goals while also laying the foundation for lifelong health and vitality.

2.2 PORTION CONTROL: THE KEY TO SUSTAINABLE WEIGHT LOSS

In the quest for sustainable weight loss, portion control stands out as one of the most practical and effective strategies. It's an approach that doesn't require you to eliminate your favorite foods or adhere to restrictive diets but instead focuses on managing the amount of food you consume. Dr. Nowzaradan's meal plan emphasizes portion control as a cornerstone for achieving and maintaining a healthy weight, empowering you to enjoy a variety of foods while still working toward your health goals.

The Power of Portion Control

In today's world, where portion sizes have steadily increased over the years, it's easy to consume more calories than our bodies need, often without even realizing it. Restaurants serve oversized meals, snacks come in larger packages, and the concept of "value" is often tied to getting more food for less money. This trend has made it difficult to gauge what an appropriate portion actually looks like, leading many to unintentionally overeat.

Portion control is about being mindful of how much you eat rather than focusing solely on what you eat. It's the art of balancing the quantity of food on your plate to meet your body's needs without exceeding them. By learning to manage portions, you can still enjoy a wide variety of foods, including those that might be considered indulgent, without derailing your weight loss efforts. This approach promotes a healthy relationship with food, where nothing is off-limits, but everything is consumed in moderation.

Understanding Hunger and Satiety

One of the first steps in mastering portion control is to reconnect with your body's natural hunger and fullness cues. In our busy lives, it's easy to eat out of habit, boredom, or emotional need rather than true hunger. Over time, this disconnect can lead to a pattern of overeating, where we consume food simply because it's available or because we feel like we should. Dr. Nowzaradan's philosophy encourages mindful eating—paying attention to when you're truly hungry and stopping when you're comfortably full. This requires slowing down during meals, savoring each bite, and allowing your body time to signal when it's had enough. It takes about 20 minutes for your brain to register fullness, so eating slowly can help prevent overeating. By tuning into your body's signals, you can better regulate your food intake and avoid the discomfort of overeating.

Practical Tips for Managing Portions

Portion control doesn't mean you have to carry a food scale everywhere you go or obsessively measure every bite. Instead, it's about adopting simple, practical habits that help you manage portion sizes naturally.

One effective strategy is to use smaller plates, bowls, and utensils. Studies have shown that people tend to eat more when they use larger dishes because the portions look smaller in comparison. By downsizing your dinnerware, you can trick your mind into feeling satisfied with less food. Similarly, using smaller utensils can help you take smaller bites, prolonging the eating experience and giving your brain more time to catch up with your stomach.

Another useful technique is to pre-portion your food before you sit down to eat. Rather than eating directly from a package or serving dish, portion out the amount you intend to eat onto your plate. This not only gives you a visual cue of how much you're consuming but also reduces the temptation to go back for seconds. For snacks, consider dividing larger packages into single-serving portions to avoid mindless munching.

When dining out, portion control can be particularly challenging, as restaurant servings are often much larger than what you need. One approach is to ask for a to-go box at the start of the meal and immediately pack away half of your dish. This way, you're not only controlling your portion size but also creating a ready-made meal for later. Alternatively, you can share a dish with a dining companion or order an appetizer as your main course to keep portions in check.

The Role of Balanced Meals

Portion control is most effective when it's combined with balanced meals that include the right mix of macronutrients—proteins, fats, and carbohydrates. Each of these nutrients plays a role in satiety, the feeling of fullness that helps you avoid overeating. Protein, for example, is known for its ability to keep you feeling full longer. Including a source of lean protein, such as chicken, fish, or beans, in every meal can help curb hunger and reduce the likelihood of snacking between meals. Fats, particularly healthy fats like those found in avocados, nuts, and olive oil, also contribute to satiety and should be included in moderation.

Carbohydrates, especially complex carbohydrates like whole grains and vegetables, provide the energy your body needs and can help regulate blood sugar levels. By including a variety of these macronutrients in each meal, you create a balanced plate that satisfies your hunger while helping you maintain portion control.

Mindful Eating and Emotional Triggers

Emotional eating is a common barrier to portion control. Many people turn to food for comfort when they're stressed, sad, or bored, leading to overeating and weight gain. Dr. Nowzaradan's plan encourages addressing the emotional aspects of eating by becoming more mindful of the reasons behind your food choices.

Mindful eating involves being present during meals, focusing on the taste, texture, and aroma of your food, and paying attention to how it makes you feel. By eating mindfully, you can better recognize when you're eating out of emotion rather than hunger and make more intentional choices about what and how much you eat.

If you find yourself reaching for food in response to stress or other emotions, it can be helpful to identify alternative coping strategies. This might include going for a walk, practicing relaxation techniques, or engaging in a hobby that distracts you from the urge to eat. By addressing the emotional triggers behind overeating, you can gain greater control over your portions and, ultimately, your weight.

Planning and Preparation

Planning and preparation are key components of successful portion control. When you have a plan in place, you're less likely to make impulsive food choices that lead to overeating. Dr. Nowzaradan's meal plan emphasizes the importance of meal planning and prepping as a way to ensure that you have healthy, portion-controlled meals ready to go.

By taking the time to plan your meals for the week, you can make intentional choices about portion sizes and ensure that your meals are balanced and satisfying. Meal prepping, where you prepare several meals or components of meals in advance, can also help you stick to your portion goals. When healthy, pre-portioned meals are readily available, you're less likely to reach for convenient, high-calorie options that sabotage your efforts.

The Long-Term Benefits of Portion Control

Mastering portion control is not just about losing weight; it's about creating sustainable eating habits that support long-term health. By learning to manage portions, you can enjoy a wide variety of foods without feeling deprived, reduce the risk of overeating, and maintain a healthy weight over time.

Dr. Nowzaradan's approach to portion control is about making mindful, informed choices that align with your health goals. It's about recognizing that you don't have to eat until you're stuffed to be satisfied and that smaller portions can be just as fulfilling when you're eating the right balance of nutrients.

As you practice portion control and integrate it into your daily routine, you'll find that it becomes second nature. You'll develop a greater awareness of your body's needs, a healthier relationship with food, and the confidence to make choices that support your well-being. In the end, portion control is not just a tool for weight loss; it's a key to sustainable, lifelong health.

In the journey toward better health and sustainable weight loss, making smart food choices is essential. One of the most effective strategies for improving your diet without feeling deprived is to swap unhealthy ingredients for more nutritious alternatives. Dr. Nowzaradan's meal plan encourages these healthy substitutions as a way to enjoy the foods you love while aligning your eating habits with your health goals. The key is to make changes that enhance the nutritional value of your meals, often without sacrificing flavor or satisfaction.

Understanding the Impact of Food Choices

Every food choice you make has a direct impact on your health, energy levels, and weight management. Many of the foods that are popular in the typical Western diet—such as refined grains, sugary snacks, and processed meats—are high in calories, unhealthy fats, and added sugars, yet low in essential nutrients. These foods can contribute to weight gain, inflammation, and the development of chronic diseases like diabetes and heart disease.

The good news is that you don't have to give up your favorite foods entirely to improve your diet. By making thoughtful substitutions, you can still enjoy the tastes and textures you crave while significantly boosting the nutritional content of your meals. This approach not only supports weight loss but also promotes long-term health by providing your body with the nutrients it needs to function optimally.

Swapping Refined Grains for Whole Grains

One of the simplest and most effective substitutions you can make is to replace refined grains with whole grains. Refined grains, like white bread, pasta, and rice, have been stripped of their fiber and many nutrients during processing, leaving behind a product that's quickly digested and can spike blood sugar levels. These spikes are often followed by crashes, leading to increased hunger and overeating. Whole grains, on the other hand, retain their fiber, vitamins, and minerals. This makes them more filling and provides a slower, more sustained release of energy. By choosing whole grain options like brown rice, whole wheat bread, quinoa, and oats, you can improve your blood sugar control, support digestive health, and reduce your risk of chronic diseases. Moreover, the fiber in whole grains helps you feel full longer, which can prevent overeating and aid in weight loss. The textures and flavors of whole grains can be just as satisfying as their refined counterparts, especially when paired with the right seasonings and ingredients.

Replacing Sugary Snacks with Natural Sweeteners

Sugar is one of the most common culprits in unhealthy eating habits. It's hidden in countless processed foods, from breakfast cereals to sauces, and consuming too much sugar can lead to weight gain, increased risk of diabetes, and other health issues. Reducing your sugar intake is a powerful way to improve your diet, and one way to do this is by swapping out sugary snacks for options that use natural sweeteners or less processed alternatives.

For instance, instead of reaching for a candy bar or a sugary granola bar, consider snacks made with whole fruits, which provide natural sweetness along with fiber, vitamins, and antioxidants. Fresh or dried fruits, when consumed in moderation, can satisfy your sweet tooth while offering significant nutritional benefits.

When baking or preparing desserts, you can also experiment with natural sweeteners like honey, maple syrup, or stevia. These alternatives often have a lower glycemic index than refined sugar, meaning they have a less dramatic effect on blood sugar levels. While it's still important to consume these sweeteners in moderation, they can be a better choice for maintaining stable energy levels and supporting overall health.

Choosing Healthy Fats Over Unhealthy Fats

Fats are an essential part of your diet, but not all fats are created equal. The type of fat you consume can significantly impact your heart health, weight management, and overall well-being. Unhealthy fats, such as trans fats and excessive saturated fats, are commonly found in processed foods, fried foods, and fatty cuts of meat. These fats can raise bad cholesterol levels, increase inflammation, and contribute to the development of heart disease.

A smarter choice is to replace unhealthy fats with healthy fats, which support heart health and provide essential fatty acids that your body needs. Healthy fats, such as those found in avocados, nuts, seeds, and olive oil, can improve cholesterol levels, reduce inflammation, and help you feel satisfied after meals. For example, instead of using butter or margarine, try cooking with olive oil or avocado oil, which are rich in monounsaturated fats. These fats are known for their heart-protective properties and can add a delicious flavor to your dishes. Similarly, replacing a snack of chips with a handful of nuts can provide healthy fats along with protein and fiber, making for a more nutritious and filling option.

Substituting Processed Meats with Lean Proteins

Processed meats, such as bacon, sausages, and deli meats, are often high in sodium, unhealthy fats, and preservatives, all of which can contribute to health issues like high blood pressure and an increased risk of certain cancers. Swapping these for leaner, more natural protein sources is a simple yet effective way to improve your diet. Lean proteins, such as chicken, turkey, fish, beans, and legumes, provide essential nutrients like protein, vitamins, and minerals without the harmful additives found in processed meats. Fish, particularly fatty fishlike salmon and mackerel, is also an excellent source of omega-3 fatty acids, which support heart and brain health. By choosing lean proteins over processed meats, you not only reduce your intake of unhealthy fats and sodium but also support muscle maintenance, which is particularly important when you're losing weight. These proteins are versatile and can be incorporated into a wide variety of dishes, ensuring that your meals remain flavorful and satisfying.

Incorporating More Vegetables

Vegetables are one of the most nutrient-dense food groups, offering a wide range of vitamins, minerals, fiber, and antioxidants with relatively few calories. Yet, many people struggle to incorporate enough vegetables into their diets. Making a conscious effort to substitute less healthy ingredients with vegetables can dramatically improve the nutritional value of your meals.

For example, you can replace some or all of the pasta in a dish with spiralized vegetables like zucchini or spaghetti squash. This not only lowers the calorie content of the meal but also adds fiber, vitamins, and a variety of phytonutrients that support health. Similarly, using lettuce leaves instead of bread or tortillas for wraps can cut down on refined carbohydrates while boosting your intake of leafy greens. Vegetables can also be used to add bulk and nutrients to soups, stews, and casseroles. By replacing some of the meat or grains in these dishes with extra vegetables, you create meals that are lower in calories but higher in vitamins, minerals, and fiber.

Making Dairy Swaps

Dairy products can be a valuable source of calcium and protein, but full-fat dairy items are also high in saturated fats. For those looking to reduce their intake of unhealthy fats or for individuals who are lactose intolerant, there are plenty of nutritious alternatives.

Swapping full-fat dairy products for low-fat or non-dairy alternatives can reduce calorie and fat intake without sacrificing flavor. For example, you can substitute whole milk with almond milk, soy milk, or another plant-based milk. These alternatives are often fortified with calcium and vitamins to match the nutritional profile of dairy milk. When it comes to yogurt, choosing Greek yogurt over regular yogurt can be a smart substitution. Greek yogurt is higher in protein and often lower in sugar, making it a more filling and health-conscious choice. For cheese, opting for varieties that are lower in fat, such as mozzarella or cottage cheese, or using smaller amounts of a strong-flavored cheese like Parmesan, can help you enjoy the taste without overdoing the saturated fat. Healthy substitutions are a powerful tool in building a balanced, nutritious diet that supports weight loss and overall health. By swapping out unhealthy ingredients for more nutritious alternatives, you can enjoy your favorite foods while enhancing their health benefits. Dr. Nowzaradan's approach to these substitutions is about making small, sustainable changes that add up to significant improvements in your diet and well-being. These swaps are not about deprivation; they're about empowerment—giving you the tools to make better choices that nourish your body, satisfy your cravings, and support your journey toward a healthier life. As you become more accustomed to these healthier alternatives, you'll find that they become second nature, transforming the way you approach food and ultimately leading to a more balanced and fulfilling relationship with eating.

CHAPTER 3: OVERCOMING COMMON DIET CHALLENGES

3.1 EMOTIONAL EATING: STRATEGIES FOR SUCCESS

Emotional eating is a challenge many people face, often without fully realizing it. When emotions—whether stress, sadness, boredom, or even happiness—trigger the urge to eat, food becomes more than just fuel for the body. It transforms into a source of comfort, a distraction, or a reward. However, while emotional eating might offer temporary relief, it often leads to a cycle of guilt, overeating, and weight gain, making it one of the most significant obstacles to achieving lasting health and weight loss.

Understanding the dynamics of emotional eating is the first step toward overcoming it. Emotional eating is not about hunger; it's about using food to cope with emotions. This behavior can become ingrained over time, often starting in childhood, where food might have been used as a reward or a way to soothe discomfort. The result is a pattern where certain emotions become tied to the act of eating, regardless of physical hunger.

Recognizing Emotional Eating Triggers

One of the most powerful tools in combating emotional eating is awareness. To change the pattern, you must first recognize the triggers that lead to emotional eating. These triggers can vary widely from person to person, but common ones include stress, anxiety, loneliness, fatigue, and even happiness. For some, the sight or smell of food can trigger an emotional response, while others might be more affected by certain situations or times of day.

To begin identifying your triggers, start by keeping a food and mood journal. Document what you eat, when you eat, and how you're feeling at the time. Over a few weeks, patterns will start to emerge. You might notice that you're more likely to reach for comfort foods after a stressful day at work, or that you tend to snack mindlessly while watching TV in the evening. This journal can become an invaluable tool in understanding the connection between your emotions and your eating habits.

Once you've identified your triggers, the next step is to explore the underlying emotions that drive your eating. Ask yourself what you're truly feeling when the urge to eat arises. Are you stressed? Lonely? Bored? Identifying the root emotion can help you address the cause of your eating, rather than just the symptom.

Developing Healthier Coping Mechanisms

The key to overcoming emotional eating is to replace unhealthy coping mechanisms with healthier ones. It's not enough to simply recognize that you're eating for emotional reasons; you need alternative strategies to manage those emotions in a more constructive way.

Stress, for example, is a common trigger for emotional eating. When stress levels rise, the body releases cortisol, a hormone that can increase appetite and lead to cravings for high-calorie, comfort foods. Instead of turning to food, find other ways to relieve stress. Physical activity is one of the most effective stress relievers. Exercise releases endorphins, which are natural mood boosters. Whether it's a brisk walk, a yoga session, or a trip to the gym, moving your body can help dissipate stress and reduce the urge to eat.

Mindfulness and relaxation techniques are also powerful tools for managing stress and emotional triggers. Practices like deep breathing, meditation, and progressive muscle relaxation can help calm your mind and body, reducing the intensity of your emotional responses. Even just a few minutes of mindfulness practice each day can help you develop a greater awareness of your emotions and create space between your feelings and your actions.

For those moments when you're feeling lonely or bored, it can be helpful to engage in activities that are mentally stimulating or socially rewarding. Call a friend, pick up a hobby, read a book, or take up a creative project. These activities can distract you from the urge to eat and provide a sense of fulfillment that food cannot offer.

Creating a Supportive Environment

Your environment plays a significant role in emotional eating. If your kitchen is stocked with junk food, or if you have easy access to unhealthy snacks, it's much harder to resist the temptation to eat when emotions run high. Creating a supportive environment is about making it easier to choose healthy behaviors over emotional eating.

Start by cleaning out your pantry and fridge, removing the foods that you're most likely to reach for when emotions strike. Replace them with healthier options—fresh fruits and vegetables, whole grains, lean proteins, and nutritious snacks that can satisfy your hunger without derailing your diet. Having these healthier choices readily available makes it easier to stick to your plan when cravings hit.

In addition to creating a physical environment that supports your goals, it's important to build a social environment that does the same. Share your challenges with friends or family members who can offer encouragement and accountability. Sometimes, just talking through your emotions with someone who understands can help alleviate the urge to eat. If you feel comfortable, consider joining a support group where others are working toward similar goals. The sense of community and shared experience can be incredibly motivating.

Practicing Self-Compassion

One of the most important aspects of overcoming emotional eating is practicing self-compassion. It's easy to fall into a cycle of guilt and self-criticism when you eat for emotional reasons. However, this negative self-talk often only reinforces the behavior, leading to more emotional eating.

Instead of beating yourself up, approach your emotional eating with curiosity and compassion. Recognize that you're human, and that changing deeply ingrained habits takes time. If you find yourself eating in response to emotions, use it as an opportunity to learn more about yourself and your triggers, rather than as a reason to feel ashamed. This shift in mindset—from judgment to understanding—can make a significant difference in your ability to make lasting changes.

Creating a Plan for Success

To successfully manage emotional eating, it's helpful to have a plan in place for when triggers arise. This plan might include a list of alternative activities to turn to when you feel the urge to eat, such as taking a walk, practicing deep breathing, or engaging in a creative hobby. You might also want to include strategies for dealing with particularly challenging situations, like social events or stressful days at work.

Additionally, it can be helpful to plan your meals and snacks ahead of time. When you know what and when you'll be eating, it's easier to stick to your plan and less likely that you'll turn to food for emotional reasons. Having healthy, balanced meals and snacks prepared in advance also ensures that you're nourishing your body in a way that supports your overall health and weight loss goals.

Emotional eating is a complex challenge, but it's one that can be overcome with awareness, healthy coping mechanisms, and self-compassion. By recognizing your triggers, developing alternative strategies for managing emotions, and creating a supportive environment, you can break the cycle of emotional eating and move toward a healthier relationship with food. Remember that this journey is about progress, not perfection. Every step you take toward understanding and managing your emotional triggers is a step toward greater health and well-being.

3.2 DINING OUT AND SOCIAL EVENTS

Dining out and attending social events are integral parts of life that bring joy, connection, and sometimes a welcome break from routine. However, when you're on a journey to improve your health and manage your weight, these occasions can present challenges. The abundance of tempting food, the social pressure to indulge, and the uncertainty of what's in the dishes being served can make it difficult to stay on track. But with the right strategies and mindset, you can navigate these situations without compromising your goals, allowing you to enjoy these moments fully while still making choices that align with your health journey.

Preparing Ahead for Success

One of the most effective ways to stay on track during dining out or social events is to plan ahead. This doesn't mean you have to know every detail of the menu or obsess over every bite, but rather that you enter the situation with a clear intention. Planning ahead gives you a sense of control and reduces the likelihood of making impulsive decisions that you might later regret.

If you know where you'll be dining, take a few minutes to look at the restaurant's menu online beforehand. Many restaurants now provide nutritional information, which can help you make informed choices. Look for dishes that are grilled, baked, or steamed rather than fried, and consider asking for dressings or sauces on the side to better manage portion sizes and calorie intake. If the restaurant doesn't have a menu available online, you can

generally assume that dishes labeled as "light," "healthy," or "heart-smart" will be better options.

For social events, especially those that involve a potluck or buffet, consider bringing a healthy dish that you enjoy. This not only ensures that there will be something you can eat without guilt but also introduces others to delicious, health-conscious options. When you arrive, survey the food choices before filling your plate. This allows you to make deliberate decisions rather than grabbing food impulsively.

Navigating the Menu

When you're at a restaurant, the menu can feel like a minefield of temptation. However, understanding how to navigate it can make all the difference. Start by identifying the healthier sections of the menu—many restaurants now have dedicated sections for lighter fare. If you're not sure what the healthiest options are, don't hesitate to ask your server for recommendations or modifications. Most restaurants are happy to accommodate requests like substituting vegetables for fries or preparing a dish with less oil.

Portion control is another important consideration when dining out. Restaurant portions are often much larger than what you would serve at home, so consider sharing an entrée with a friend or asking for a to-go box at the start of the meal and packing away half your dish for later. This allows you to enjoy your meal without overeating and provides you with a delicious second serving to enjoy another time.

Another tip is to be mindful of beverages. Drinks can add a significant number of calories to your meal, especially if they're sugary or alcoholic. Opt for water, sparkling water with a slice of lemon, or unsweetened tea. If you choose to have an alcoholic beverage, consider a wine spritzer or a light beer, and limit yourself to one drink to keep your calorie intake in check.

Handling Social Pressures

Social events often come with their own set of pressures—whether it's the insistence of a host who's proud of their cooking or the casual encouragement of friends to indulge. It's important to remember that you're in control of your choices, and it's okay to politely decline or set boundaries that align with your goals.

One strategy is to be upfront about your dietary goals with those you trust. Letting your friends or family know that you're focusing on healthier eating can garner their support rather than their pressure. Often, they'll be more understanding than you might expect, and some may even join you in making healthier choices.

When someone offers you food that you'd prefer not to eat, a simple, polite refusal can go a long way. You might say, "That looks delicious, but I'm really full right now," or "I'm trying to stick to my plan, but I appreciate the offer." If you feel comfortable, you can even share a bit about your health journey and why certain foods aren't part of your plan at the moment.

If the event is one where food is a central focus, such as a holiday dinner or a celebratory feast, consider the "three-bite rule." This approach allows you to enjoy a small portion of a tempting dish without going overboard. Savor the first bite, enjoy the second, and then decide if you're satisfied after the third. Often, this mindful approach allows you to enjoy the flavors without the need for a full serving.

Focusing on the Experience

It's easy to get caught up in the food at social events, but these occasions are really about the connections we make and the experiences we share. Shifting your focus away from the food and toward the people and conversations around you can help reduce the pressure to eat.

Try to engage in activities that don't revolve around food. If you're at a party, spend time mingling, dancing, or participating in games. If you're at a family gathering, offer to help with something that doesn't involve eating, like setting up or organizing an activity. By focusing on the social aspect of the event, you can enjoy the occasion fully without making food the central attraction.

Managing Expectations and Enjoying the Moment

Perfection isn't the goal; balance is. It's important to give yourself permission to enjoy the foods you love, even if they're not the healthiest options. The key is to do so mindfully and without guilt. If you indulge in a favorite dish, savor it, enjoy it, and then move on. One meal, one dish, or one event won't derail your progress as long as it's part of a balanced approach to eating.

It's also helpful to set realistic expectations for yourself. There will be times when you eat more than you planned, and that's okay. The important thing is how you respond afterward. Instead of feeling guilty or giving up, use it as an opportunity to refocus on your goals and get back on track at your next meal. Remember, health is a lifelong journey, not a short-term endeavor.

Dining out and attending social events don't have to be obstacles to your health goals. With a bit of planning, mindfulness, and a focus on the experience rather than just the food, you can enjoy these occasions without sacrificing your progress. Dr. Nowzaradan's approach is all about balance—allowing you to live your life fully while making choices that support your health and well-being. By developing these strategies, you'll find that staying on track is not only possible but also enjoyable, allowing you to savor both the food and the moments that matter most.

3.3 DEALING WITH PLATEAUS

Weight loss is often described as a journey, and like any journey, it comes with its own set of challenges. One of the most frustrating obstacles many people encounter is the dreaded plateau. After weeks or even months of steady progress, the scale suddenly stops moving, despite your continued efforts. This can be discouraging, but it's important to understand that plateaus are a natural part of the weight loss process. They don't signify failure; rather, they signal that it's time to make some adjustments and push through to the next phase of your journey.

Understanding Why Plateaus Happen

To overcome a plateau, it's helpful to first understand why they occur. As you lose weight, your body undergoes various changes. Your metabolism slows down because your body requires fewer calories to maintain a smaller frame. Additionally, your body becomes more efficient at the physical activities you regularly perform, meaning you burn fewer calories during exercise. These factors can combine to create a plateau, where the calories you're burning no longer exceed the calories you're consuming, halting further weight loss.

Another reason for plateaus can be related to muscle mass. As you lose fat, you might also be gaining muscle, especially if you're incorporating strength training into your routine. Since muscle is denser than fat, your weight might remain the same or even increase slightly, despite continued fat loss. This can be misleading if you're only tracking progress by the scale, making it seem like you've hit a plateau when, in reality, your body composition is improving.

Reassessing Your Diet

When you hit a plateau, it's an opportunity to take a closer look at your diet. Over time, it's easy for portion sizes to creep up or for small indulgences to become more frequent. What once worked may no longer be enough to keep you in a calorie deficit.

Start by tracking your food intake more diligently for a week or two. This can help you identify any changes in your eating habits that might be contributing to the plateau. Are you eating more than you realize? Are you consuming hidden calories in the form of snacks, beverages, or condiments? Once you've identified potential areas for improvement, make adjustments to bring your calorie intake back in line with your goals. You might also consider incorporating more nutrient-dense, lower-calorie foods into your diet. Foods high in fiber, such as vegetables, fruits, and whole grains, can help you feel full and satisfied while consuming fewer calories. Additionally, lean proteins can support muscle maintenance and repair, helping you preserve muscle mass while continuing to lose fat.

Shaking Up Your Exercise Routine

Just as your body adapts to your diet, it can also adapt to your exercise routine. If you've been doing the same workouts for a while, your body becomes more efficient at performing them, leading to fewer calories burned. This is a common reason for hitting a plateau. To break through, consider varying your workouts. This could mean increasing the intensity, duration, or frequency of your exercise sessions. If you've been focusing primarily on cardio, try incorporating strength training, which can help build muscle and boost your metabolism. Conversely, if your routine has been heavily strength-based, adding more cardio can help increase your calorie burn.

High-intensity interval training (HIIT) is another effective strategy for overcoming plateaus. HIIT involves alternating between short bursts of intense activity and periods of lower-intensity exercise or rest. This type of training has been shown to burn more calories in a shorter amount of time and can be a powerful tool for breaking through a plateau.

Monitoring Non-Scale Victories

While the number on the scale is one way to measure progress, it's not the only indicator of success. During a plateau, it's important to focus on other signs of improvement, often referred to as "non-scale victories." These can include how your clothes fit, your energy levels, your strength and endurance, and even your overall sense of well-being.

Take time to acknowledge and celebrate these victories. You might notice that you're stronger, more flexible, or have greater stamina than you did at the start of your journey. Perhaps you've developed healthier eating habits or a more positive relationship with food. These are significant achievements that contribute to your long-term health, even if the scale isn't reflecting them immediately.

Shifting your focus from weight alone to overall health and wellness can help you stay motivated during a plateau. Remember that the ultimate goal is not just to lose weight, but to build a healthier, more vibrant life.

Staying Positive and Patient

Plateaus can be frustrating, but they're also a sign that you're on the right track. Your body is adjusting to the changes you've made, and with persistence, you can push through to the next phase of your journey. It's important to stay positive and patient during this time. Weight loss is rarely a linear process, and everyone experiences plateaus at some point.

Instead of seeing a plateau as a setback, view it as an opportunity to refine your approach and make necessary adjustments. This might involve tweaking your diet, changing up your exercise routine, or simply giving your body time to adjust. Trust the process, and remember that consistency is key. Even if progress seems slow, the healthy habits you've developed will continue to benefit you in the long run.

Seeking Support

Sometimes, breaking through a plateau requires a little extra support. This could mean working with a fitness coach, a dietitian, or even just reaching out to a friend who's on a similar journey. Having someone to talk to can provide valuable insights, motivation, and accountability.

Support groups, whether online or in person, can also be a great resource. Sharing your experiences with others who understand the challenges of weight loss can offer encouragement and new perspectives. Sometimes, just knowing that you're not alone in your struggle can make all the difference.

Dealing with plateaus is a natural part of any weight loss journey. While they can be discouraging, they're also an opportunity to reassess, adjust, and renew your commitment to your goals. By understanding why plateaus happen, making strategic changes to your diet and exercise routine, and focusing on non-scale victories, you can push through these periods of stagnation and continue making progress.

Remember, the journey to better health is not a sprint; it's a marathon. Plateaus are just one of the many challenges you'll face along the way. With patience, persistence, and the right strategies, you can overcome them and move closer to achieving the healthy, vibrant life you deserve.

CHAPTER 4: INTEGRATING FITNESS WITH YOUR MEAL PLAN

4.1 EXERCISE ESSENTIALS

Physical activity is a cornerstone of health, and when combined with a balanced meal plan, it becomes a powerful tool for achieving and maintaining weight loss, enhancing overall well-being, and improving quality of life. While nutrition provides the essential fuel your body needs, exercise is the mechanism that uses that fuel to build strength, increase endurance, and maintain a healthy metabolism. Dr. Nowzaradan's approach to weight loss emphasizes the importance of integrating regular physical activity with your meal plan to achieve the best possible results.

The Synergy Between Diet and Exercise

Diet and exercise are often viewed as separate components of a healthy lifestyle, but in reality, they are deeply interconnected. What you eat fuels your body's movements, and how you move influences your body's nutritional needs. When these elements are balanced, they create a synergistic effect that enhances weight loss and overall health.

Exercise increases the number of calories your body burns, which is essential for creating the calorie deficit needed for weight loss. But beyond just burning calories, exercise has numerous other benefits that support your weight loss journey. It helps preserve lean muscle mass, which is crucial because muscle burns more calories at rest than fat. This means that the more muscle you have, the higher your resting metabolic rate, and the more calories you'll burn even when you're not exercising.

Moreover, physical activity boosts your body's sensitivity to insulin, helping to regulate blood sugar levels more effectively. This is particularly important for those who are at risk of or are managing conditions like type 2 diabetes. Exercise also promotes better digestion and improves sleep quality—both of which are critical for weight management and overall health.

The Psychological Benefits of Exercise

The benefits of exercise extend beyond the physical. Regular physical activity is a powerful tool for managing stress, reducing anxiety, and combating depression. When you exercise, your body releases endorphins, often referred to as "feel-good" hormones. These natural chemicals improve your mood, increase your sense of well-being, and can even create a feeling of euphoria commonly known as the "runner's high."

Incorporating exercise into your routine can also boost your self-esteem and confidence. As you become stronger, fitter, and more capable, you'll likely find that you feel better about your body and your abilities. This positive self-perception can reinforce healthy behaviors and make it easier to stick to your meal plan and exercise regimen over the long term.

Exercise also provides a constructive outlet for emotions. Many people struggle with emotional eating, using food as a way to cope with stress or negative feelings. By engaging in regular physical activity, you can develop healthier ways to manage emotions, reducing the reliance on food for comfort.

Finding the Right Type of Exercise

When it comes to exercise, there is no one-size-fits-all approach. The best type of exercise is the one that you enjoy and can commit to doing regularly. It's important to find activities that fit your lifestyle, preferences, and fitness level, as this will increase the likelihood that you'll stick with them.

For some, this might mean going for daily walks, which can be as effective as more intense forms of exercise when done consistently. Walking is a low-impact, accessible form of exercise that can be easily integrated into your daily routine. Whether it's a brisk walk around your neighborhood, a hike in nature, or even just taking the stairs instead of the elevator, walking is a simple yet effective way to get moving.

Others might prefer activities like swimming, cycling, or dancing—forms of exercise that are not only great for cardiovascular health but also fun and enjoyable. If you enjoy what you're doing, it won't feel like a chore, and you'll be more motivated to keep it up.

Strength training is another critical component of a balanced exercise routine, particularly when combined with a weight loss plan. Lifting weights or doing bodyweight exercises like push-ups, squats, and lunges helps build muscle, which in turn increases your metabolism. Strength training also improves bone density, enhances joint stability, and helps prevent injuries, making it an important part of a well-rounded fitness regimen.

Overcoming Barriers to Exercise

Even with the best intentions, many people find it challenging to incorporate regular exercise into their lives. Time constraints, lack of motivation, and physical limitations are common barriers that can make it difficult to stay active.

If time is an issue, consider breaking up your exercise into shorter, more manageable sessions. You don't need to spend hours at the gym to reap the benefits of physical activity. Even 10-15 minutes of exercise, done a few times a day, can add up and make a significant difference. High-intensity interval training (HIIT) is a great option for those with limited time. These short, intense bursts of activity followed by brief periods of rest can provide a full workout in as little as 20-30 minutes.

For those struggling with motivation, finding a workout buddy or joining a group class can help. Exercising with others not only provides accountability but also makes the experience more enjoyable. Additionally, setting small, achievable goals can help keep you motivated. Celebrate each milestone, whether it's completing a certain number of workouts in a week, lifting a heavier weight, or walking a little farther than before. These successes, no matter how small, can build momentum and keep you moving forward.

Physical limitations, such as chronic pain or mobility issues, can also be a barrier to exercise. However, it's important to remember that any movement is better than none. If traditional forms of exercise are difficult, look for alternatives that suit your abilities. Water-based exercises, chair exercises, or gentle yoga are all excellent options for those with physical limitations. It's also advisable to consult with a healthcare provider or a fitness professional who can help you design a safe and effective exercise plan tailored to your needs.

Integrating Exercise with Your Meal Plan

To maximize the benefits of exercise, it's important to integrate it with your meal plan. Proper nutrition fuels your workouts and aids in recovery, while exercise helps you make the most of the nutrients you consume.

Before exercise, focus on meals that provide sustained energy. Complex carbohydrates, such as whole grains, paired with lean protein, can provide the fuel your body needs for a good workout. After exercise, prioritize protein-rich foods to support muscle repair and recovery. Hydration is also key—make sure to drink plenty of water before, during, and after your workouts to stay properly hydrated.

Listening to your body is crucial. If you're feeling fatigued or run down, it may be a sign that you need to adjust your diet or exercise routine. Balancing exercise with adequate rest and proper nutrition will help you avoid burnout and injury, ensuring that you can maintain your physical activity in the long term.

Exercise is an essential component of a healthy lifestyle, especially when combined with a balanced meal plan. It enhances weight loss, supports mental and emotional well-being, and contributes to overall health in ways that go beyond the scale. By finding activities you enjoy, overcoming barriers, and integrating exercise with proper nutrition, you can harness the full power of physical activity to achieve better health and a more vibrant life. Remember, the goal is not just to lose weight, but to build a stronger, healthier, and more resilient body that can carry you through all the challenges and joys that life has to offer.

4.2 TIME-EFFICIENT WORKOUTS FOR BUSY LIVES

In today's fast-paced world, finding time for exercise can feel like a daunting challenge. Between work, family, and other responsibilities, it's easy to let physical activity fall to the bottom of the priority list. However, regular exercise is crucial not only for weight loss but also for overall health and well-being. The good news is that you don't need hours in the gym to see results. With the right approach, short, time-efficient workouts can be just as effective as longer sessions, especially when they're paired with a balanced meal plan.

The Importance of Efficiency in Workouts

When time is limited, it's all about maximizing efficiency. The key to effective, time-efficient workouts is to focus on intensity and full-body movements that engage multiple muscle groups at once. This not only helps you burn more calories in less time but also ensures that you're getting a balanced workout that improves strength, cardiovascular health, and endurance.

High-intensity interval training (HIIT) is one of the most popular and effective methods for those with busy schedules. HIIT involves alternating between short bursts of intense activity and periods of rest or lower-intensity exercise. These workouts can be completed in as little as 20-30 minutes, making them perfect for fitting into a busy day. Despite their short duration, HIIT workouts are highly effective at burning calories, boosting metabolism, and improving cardiovascular fitness.

Another approach is to incorporate circuit training, which involves moving quickly from one exercise to the next with minimal rest in between. Circuit training combines strength and cardio exercises, allowing you to build muscle while also getting your heart rate up. This type of workout can be done in 20-30 minutes and provides a comprehensive fitness routine that covers all the bases.

Creating a Time-Efficient Workout Routine

Designing a time-efficient workout routine doesn't have to be complicated. The goal is to create a balanced plan that targets all major muscle groups while also getting your heart rate up. Here's a general framework that you can adapt to your preferences and fitness level:

1. Warm-Up (3-5 minutes):

Start with a brief warm-up to get your blood flowing and prepare your muscles for exercise. This could include marching in place, light jogging, or dynamic stretches like arm circles and leg swings. Warming up reduces the risk of injury and helps you get the most out of your workout.

2. HIIT or Circuit Training (15-20 minutes):

Choose a combination of exercises that target different muscle groups. For example, you might alternate between bodyweight exercises like squats, push-ups, and lunges, and cardio movements like jumping jacks, high knees, or burpees. Perform each exercise for 30-45 seconds, followed by 15-30 seconds of rest before moving on to the next exercise. Repeat the circuit 2-3 times, depending on how much time you have.

3. Strength Training Focus (5-10 minutes):

If you have time, add a few focused strength exercises to build muscle in specific areas. This could include exercises like planks for core strength, dumbbell curls for arms, or glute bridges for lower body strength. Focus on maintaining good form and performing each movement with control.

4. Cool-Down (2-3 minutes):

End your workout with a cool-down period to gradually lower your heart rate and stretch your muscles. This could include gentle stretching or deep breathing exercises. Cooling down helps prevent dizziness and promotes recovery.

Making the Most of Your Time

Even with the most time-efficient workout routine, consistency is key. It's better to do short workouts regularly than to aim for long sessions that you struggle to fit in. Here are some tips for staying consistent with your workouts, even on the busiest days:

1. Schedule Your Workouts:

Treat your workouts like any other important appointment. Block out time in your calendar and stick to it. Whether it's first thing in the morning, during a lunch break, or in the evening after work, finding a regular time that works for you will help make exercise a habit.

2. Break It Up:

If finding a solid block of time is difficult, consider breaking your workout into smaller sessions throughout the day. For example, you might do a 10-minute workout in the morning and another 10-minute session in the evening. These mini-workouts can add up and still provide significant health benefits.

3. Combine Exercise with Other Activities:

Look for opportunities to incorporate physical activity into your daily routine. This could mean taking a walk during a conference call, doing a quick set of squats

while waiting for your coffee to brew, or stretching while watching TV. Small bursts of activity throughout the day can contribute to your overall fitness.

4. Use Technology to Your Advantage:

There are countless fitness apps and online videos designed for short, effective workouts that you can do at home with minimal equipment. Many of these programs offer guided routines that take the guesswork out of your workout and help you stay motivated. Having a workout plan ready to go can make it easier to get started, especially when time is tight.

The Benefits of Short, Intense Workouts

One of the biggest advantages of time-efficient workouts is their ability to fit seamlessly into your life. These workouts require minimal time commitment while still providing a full-body workout that supports your health goals. Additionally, short, intense workouts can be more sustainable over the long term, as they're easier to maintain than longer sessions that may feel overwhelming.

Short workouts also help improve cardiovascular health, boost metabolism, and enhance mood. The intensity of these sessions helps release endorphins, which can reduce stress and improve mental clarity—benefits that are particularly valuable when you're balancing a busy schedule.

Moreover, when combined with a balanced meal plan, these workouts can accelerate weight loss and improve body composition. The increase in muscle mass from strength training boosts your metabolism, helping you burn more calories even at rest. Meanwhile, the cardiovascular component helps improve heart health and endurance.

Overcoming Common Challenges

Despite the many benefits of time-efficient workouts, it's normal to encounter challenges along the way. Common obstacles include lack of motivation, fatigue, and finding the energy to work out after a long day.

Here are some strategies to overcome these challenges:

1. Set Clear Goals:

Having a clear goal can provide motivation and direction. Whether your goal is to lose weight, build strength, or simply feel better, keep it in mind as you plan your workouts. Celebrate small victories along the way to stay motivated.

2. Be Flexible:

Life is unpredictable, and sometimes plans change. If you miss a workout, don't stress. Instead, adjust your schedule and get back on track as soon as possible. Flexibility is key to maintaining a long-term fitness routine.

3. Focus on Quality Over Quantity:

When time is limited, focus on the quality of your movements rather than the duration of your workout. Performing exercises with proper form and intensity will yield better results than rushing through a longer session.

Incorporating time-efficient workouts into your routine is an excellent way to stay active and healthy, even with a busy schedule. These short, effective routines can complement your meal plan and help you achieve your fitness goals without requiring hours of exercise each day. By focusing on intensity, consistency, and making the most of your time, you can enjoy the many benefits of regular physical activity while balancing the demands of daily life. Remember, every bit of movement counts, and with the right approach, you can make exercise a sustainable part of your life, no matter how busy you are.

4.3 TRACKING YOUR PROGRESS

Tracking your progress is an essential part of any fitness and dietary plan. It not only provides tangible evidence of your achievements but also helps keep you motivated, focused, and accountable. When you can see the results of your hard work, it reinforces the positive habits you're building and encourages you to keep moving forward. Dr. Nowzaradan's approach to integrating fitness with your meal plan emphasizes the importance of monitoring your progress to ensure that you're on the right track and making the adjustments necessary to continue your journey toward better health.

The Importance of Tracking Progress

Tracking your progress allows you to measure the effectiveness of your efforts, identify what's working, and pinpoint areas that may need improvement. It also helps you stay motivated by showing you how far you've come, even when the changes might not be immediately visible. For example, while the number on the scale might not shift dramatically from week to week, other indicators—like increased strength, improved endurance, or changes in body measurements—can reveal that you're making significant strides.

Moreover, tracking progress isn't just about recording successes. It also helps you identify patterns or obstacles that might be hindering your progress. By keeping a detailed record of your diet, exercise, and other lifestyle factors, you can gain insights into what might be causing plateaus or setbacks, allowing you to make informed decisions about how to adjust your plan.

Tools for Tracking Fitness Progress

There are many tools available to help you track your fitness progress, ranging from simple to high-tech. The key is to choose the methods that best suit your lifestyle and goals, making it easy and convenient to monitor your achievements.

1. Fitness Journals:

A fitness journal is a straightforward and effective way to track your workouts. In your journal, you can record the exercises you perform, the number of sets and repetitions, the amount of weight lifted, and any other relevant details. Over time, this will allow you to see how your strength, endurance, and overall fitness are improving. Journaling also provides a space to reflect on how you feel before, during, and after your workouts, which can help you better understand the impact of exercise on your body and mind.

2. Wearable Fitness Trackers:

Wearable devices like fitness trackers and smartwatches have become increasingly popular for monitoring physical activity. These devices can track a wide range of metrics, including steps taken, calories burned, heart rate, and sleep patterns. Many also allow you to set goals, such as a daily step count or a certain number of active minutes per day, and provide reminders to keep you on track. The data collected by these devices can be synced with apps that analyze your progress over time, offering a comprehensive view of your fitness journey.

3. Mobile Apps:

There is countless fitness apps designed to help you track your workouts and monitor your progress. Some apps are specifically geared toward certain types of exercise, such as running, cycling, or strength training, while others offer more general tracking capabilities. Many of these apps allow you to set goals, log your workouts, and even connect with friends or a community for added motivation. They can also provide visual representations of your progress, such as charts or graphs, which can be incredibly motivating.

4. Progress Photos:

Sometimes, the changes in your body composition are best captured through progress photos. Taking photos at regular intervals, such as once a month, allows you to visually compare your body's transformation over time. It's a powerful way to see the results of your efforts, especially when the scale isn't showing a significant change. Make sure to take your photos under similar conditions each time—such as in the same lighting, wearing the same clothing, and from the same angles—to get the most accurate comparisons.

Tools for Tracking Dietary Progress

Just as with fitness, tracking your dietary progress is crucial for achieving your health goals. It helps ensure that you're staying within your calorie and macronutrient targets, making healthy choices, and adjusting your diet as needed.

1. Food Journals:

Keeping a food journal is one of the most effective ways to monitor your eating habits. In your journal, record everything you eat and drink throughout the day, including portion sizes and any relevant nutritional information. This practice not only helps you stay accountable but also allows you to identify patterns, such as emotional eating or snacking late at night. Over time, you can use this information to make adjustments to your diet that support your goals.

2. Mobile Apps for Nutrition Tracking:

There are numerous apps available that make tracking your dietary intake easier than ever. These apps typically allow you to log your meals and snacks, providing detailed nutritional information, including calories, macronutrients, and micronutrients. Some apps even have barcode scanners that make it simple to enter packaged foods. These tools can help you stay within your daily targets and provide insights into how your diet is impacting your progress.

3. Portion Control Tools:

For those who struggle with portion sizes, using tools like measuring cups, food scales, or portion control plates can be incredibly helpful. These tools ensure that you're eating the right amounts of each food group, helping you stay on track with your calorie and macronutrient goals. Over time, as you become more familiar with appropriate portion sizes, you may find that you can rely less on these tools and more on your intuition.

Combining Fitness and Dietary Tracking

To get the most out of your tracking efforts, it's important to combine fitness and dietary tracking into a cohesive strategy. By monitoring both aspects of your health journey, you can see how they influence each other and make more informed decisions.

For example, you might notice that on days when you skip breakfast, your workouts feel more challenging, or that increasing your protein intake helps you recover more quickly after strength training. These insights can help you fine-tune your meal plan and exercise routine to better support your goals.

Staying Motivated Through Tracking

One of the greatest benefits of tracking your progress is the motivation it provides. Seeing tangible evidence of your efforts—whether it's an increase in the weight you can lift, a decrease in body measurements, or simply feeling more energetic—can be incredibly empowering. It reinforces the connection between your actions and results, helping you stay committed to your journey.

However, it's important to approach tracking with a positive mindset. Instead of focusing solely on the numbers, consider how tracking can help you celebrate your successes, identify areas for improvement, and maintain balance in your approach. Remember that progress isn't always linear—there will be ups and downs along the way. By keeping a long-term perspective and using tracking as a tool for self-awareness and growth, you can stay motivated and continue making strides toward your goals.

Tracking your fitness and dietary progress is a vital component of a successful health and wellness plan. It provides the insights you need to make informed decisions, stay accountable, and celebrate your achievements. Whether you use a simple journal, high-tech gadgets, or a combination of methods, the key is consistency. By regularly monitoring your progress, you'll be better equipped to stay on track, overcome challenges, and continue your journey toward a healthier, more vibrant life. Remember, every small step counts, and by tracking your progress, you're investing in your future well-being.

CHAPTER 5: SUSTAINING LONG-TERM SUCCESS

5.1 MAINTAINING YOUR WEIGHT LOSS

Achieving your weight loss goals is a significant milestone, but the journey doesn't end there. The challenge many people face is maintaining that hard-earned weight loss over the long term. Keeping the weight off requires a shift in mindset—from focusing solely on losing pounds to sustaining a healthy lifestyle that supports your new weight and overall well-being. Dr. Nowzaradan's approach to long-term success emphasizes the importance of building habits that are not only effective but also sustainable. By adopting strategies that fit seamlessly into your life, you can maintain your weight loss and continue to thrive.

Understanding the Maintenance Mindset

One of the most critical aspects of maintaining weight loss is developing the right mindset. While the weight loss phase may have been characterized by more structured eating plans and rigorous exercise routines, maintenance is about finding a balance that you can sustain indefinitely. This doesn't mean you abandon the principles that helped you lose weight; rather, it means adjusting them to fit your new reality.

Maintaining weight loss requires a mindset shift from short-term goals to long-term habits. It's about recognizing that the strategies that worked for you during weight loss are now part of your daily life. This includes continuing to eat mindfully, staying active, and monitoring your progress. By embracing these habits as part of your identity rather than a temporary phase, you'll be more likely to sustain your success.

Building Sustainable Eating Habits

A key to maintaining weight loss is finding an eating pattern that supports your new weight without feeling restrictive. This often involves making small adjustments to your diet to accommodate your current calorie needs, which are likely lower than they were during the weight loss phase.

One effective strategy is to continue focusing on whole, nutrient-dense foods that provide the vitamins, minerals, and energy your body needs. These foods help you feel satisfied and energized, making it easier to avoid the pitfalls of overeating. However, it's also important to allow yourself flexibility. Enjoying your favorite foods in moderation can prevent feelings of deprivation and help you stay on track.

Mindful eating remains a powerful tool in the maintenance phase. Paying attention to hunger and fullness cues, eating slowly, and savoring your meals can prevent overeating and help you maintain a healthy relationship with food. Additionally, keeping portion sizes in check is crucial. It's easy to slip back into old habits, so continue to be mindful of the amounts you're consuming.

Another important aspect of maintaining weight loss is being prepared for the occasional indulgence. Life is full of celebrations, holidays, and social events where food plays a central role. Instead of feeling guilty about enjoying these moments, plan for them. Balance an indulgent meal with lighter choices before or after, and focus on the overall quality of your diet rather than any single meal.

Staying Active for Life

Physical activity plays a crucial role in maintaining weight loss. While exercise was likely a significant part of your weight loss journey, it's just as important in the maintenance phase. Regular physical activity helps you burn calories, maintain muscle mass, and keep your metabolism active. It also contributes to overall health, reducing the risk of chronic diseases and improving mood and mental well-being.

The key to staying active for life is finding activities you enjoy. Whether it's walking, cycling, swimming, or dancing, choose exercises that you look forward to and that fit into your lifestyle. Variety is also important—mixing up your routine can prevent boredom and ensure that you're working different muscle groups.

Incorporating physical activity into your daily routine is one of the best ways to stay consistent. This could mean taking the stairs instead of the elevator, walking or biking to work, or scheduling regular workouts at a time that works best for you. The goal is to make movement a natural and enjoyable part of your day, rather than something you have to force yourself to do.

Strength training is particularly beneficial during the maintenance phase. Building and maintaining muscle mass is crucial for keeping your metabolism active, as muscle tissue burns more calories at rest than fat tissue. Aim to include strength training exercises at least two to three times a week, focusing on all major muscle groups.

Monitoring Your Progress

Regularly monitoring your progress is essential for maintaining weight loss. This doesn't mean obsessively weighing yourself every day, but rather keeping an eye on the trends over time. Weighing yourself weekly or biweekly can help you stay aware of any changes and allow you to make adjustments if needed.

In addition to the scale, consider other ways to monitor your progress. This could include taking body measurements, tracking your fitness levels, or simply paying attention to how your clothes fit. These indicators can provide a more comprehensive view of your progress and help you stay motivated.

Journaling can also be a valuable tool in the maintenance phase. Keeping a record of your meals, workouts, and how you're feeling can help you identify patterns and stay accountable. It's also a great way to celebrate your successes and reflect on how far you've come.

Navigating Challenges and Setbacks

Maintenance is not without its challenges. Life is unpredictable, and there will be times when you face stress, changes in routine, or other factors that can make it difficult to stay on track. The important thing is to approach these challenges with a mindset of resilience and flexibility.

If you find yourself slipping back into old habits or regaining some weight, don't panic. Instead, take it as a sign that you may need to revisit your strategies and make some adjustments. Reflect on what's changed and consider how you can adapt your plan to better fit your current situation. Remember, setbacks are a normal part of any long-term journey, and they don't mean you've failed.

Having a support system in place can make a big difference when navigating challenges. Whether it's friends, family, a support group, or a healthcare professional, having people you can turn to for encouragement and advice can help you stay motivated and on track.

Embracing the Journey

Finally, maintaining weight loss is about embracing the journey rather than focusing solely on the destination. It's about recognizing that the habits you've built are not just for a set period, but for life. By viewing maintenance as an ongoing process of learning, growing, and adapting, you'll be better equipped to sustain your success.

Celebrate the progress you've made and take pride in the healthy lifestyle you've created. By staying committed to your habits, remaining flexible in your approach, and continuing to prioritize your health, you'll be able to maintain your weight loss and enjoy the benefits of a vibrant, healthy life for years to come. Remember, the journey doesn't end with weight loss—it's just the beginning of a new chapter in your health and well-being.

5.2 MANAGING CRAVINGS AND AVOIDING RELAPSE

Maintaining long-term success in your weight loss journey requires more than just adhering to a diet and exercise routine; it demands a deeper understanding of how to manage cravings and avoid relapse into old habits. Cravings can be one of the most challenging aspects of maintaining a healthy lifestyle. They can arise unexpectedly, triggered by stress, emotions, or even certain environments. Learning how to manage these cravings and prevent diet backslides is crucial for sustaining your progress and continuing on your path to better health.

Understanding Cravings

Cravings are more than just a desire for a specific food; they often have emotional or psychological roots. They can be triggered by stress, boredom, habits, or even social situations. Understanding the underlying causes of your cravings is the first step in managing them effectively.

For many people, cravings are linked to certain emotional states. Stress, anxiety, and even happiness can trigger a desire for comfort foods—those high in sugar, fat, or salt. These foods often provide a temporary sense of relief or pleasure, but they can lead to feelings of guilt or frustration if they derail your health goals.

Another common cause of cravings is habit. If you're used to having a snack at a particular time of day, your body and mind may expect it, even if you're not truly hungry. Similarly, certain environments—like the smell of popcorn at a movie theater—can trigger a craving because your brain associates that setting with eating.

Recognizing these triggers is essential for managing cravings. By identifying the situations, emotions, or habits that lead to cravings, you can develop strategies to address them before they lead to unhealthy eating choices.

Strategies for Managing Cravings

Once you understand what triggers your cravings, the next step is to develop strategies to manage them. The goal isn't necessarily to eliminate cravings completely—after all, cravings are a natural part of life—but to control how you respond to them.

1. Delay and Distract:

One of the most effective ways to manage a craving is to delay acting on it. Cravings often pass within 20 to 30 minutes if you can distract yourself with another activity. When a craving strikes, try engaging in something that takes your mind off food. This could be going for a walk, calling a friend, reading a book, or even doing a quick workout. By the time you're finished, the craving may have diminished or disappeared entirely.

2. Drink Water:

Sometimes, what we perceive as hunger or a craving is actually thirst. The body's signals for hunger and thirst can be similar, so drinking a glass of water when a craving hits can help determine if you're truly hungry. If you're still craving something after hydrating, then it may be time to address it in a healthier way.

3. Opt for a Healthy Substitute:

If a craving persists, consider finding a healthier alternative that satisfies your desire without derailing your diet. For example, if you're craving something sweet, a piece of fruit might do the trick. If you're longing for something salty, try a handful of nuts or seeds instead of chips. The key is to find a substitute that offers some nutritional value while still addressing the craving.

4. Practice Mindful Eating:

Mindful eating is about being fully present during meals, paying attention to the taste, texture, and satisfaction that food provides. When a craving hits, take a moment to consider whether you're truly hungry or if something else is driving your desire to eat. If you choose to indulge, do so mindfully—enjoy each bite slowly, and focus on the experience. This can help you feel more satisfied with a smaller portion, reducing the likelihood of overeating.

Preventing Diet Backslides

Even with the best intentions, everyone experiences setbacks from time to time. The important thing is not to let a slip turn into a slide. Preventing diet backslides involves maintaining perspective, staying flexible, and being prepared to get back on track.

1. Don't Dwell on Slip-Ups:

If you do give in to a craving or find yourself eating more than planned, it's important not to dwell on it. One indulgent meal or snack isn't going to undo all of your progress. Instead of beating yourself up, acknowledge what happened, identify any triggers, and move on. The sooner you get back to your healthy habits, the less impact the slip-up will have.

2. Stay Flexible:

Rigid dieting can lead to feelings of deprivation, which often triggers cravings and binge eating. Instead of sticking to a strict, inflexible plan, allow yourself some leeway. If you know you're going to have a special treat or meal, plan for it. Balance it with healthier choices throughout the day, and enjoy it without guilt. Flexibility in your diet helps you maintain a healthy relationship with food and reduces the risk of feeling deprived.

3. Plan for Temptations:

Being prepared is one of the best ways to prevent backslides. If you know you're going to be in a situation where temptations will be high—like a party, holiday gathering, or a night out—plan ahead. Eat a healthy snack before you go, so you're not overly hungry, and set some boundaries for yourself, such as limiting alcohol or desserts. Having a plan in place makes it easier to stay on track.

4. Focus on the Big Picture:

Weight maintenance is a marathon, not a sprint. It's natural to have ups and downs along the way. The key is to keep the big picture in mind. Focus on your long-term goals, and don't let one bad day derail your entire plan. Remember why you started your journey in the first place, and use that motivation to stay committed.

Building a Support System

Managing cravings and preventing relapse isn't something you have to do alone. Building a strong support system can make all the difference. Whether it's friends, family, a support group, or a healthcare professional, having people you can turn to for encouragement, advice, and accountability can help you stay on track.

Sharing your challenges with others who understand what you're going through can provide a sense of community and reduce the feelings of isolation that can sometimes accompany a weight loss journey. Your support system can also offer practical advice for managing cravings, staying motivated, and getting back on track after a setback.

Managing cravings and avoiding relapse are essential components of sustaining long-term success in your weight loss journey. By understanding your cravings, developing strategies to manage them, and building a strong support system, you can maintain your progress and continue to lead a healthy, fulfilling life. Remember, cravings are a natural part of life, but how you respond to them makes all the difference. By staying mindful, flexible, and focused on your long-term goals, you can keep cravings in check and prevent them from derailing your success.

5.3 PLANNING FOR SPECIAL OCCASIONS AND HOLIDAYS

Special occasions and holidays are often synonymous with indulgent meals, festive treats, and a break from the usual routine. While these events bring joy and create lasting memories, they can also present challenges for those committed to maintaining a healthy lifestyle. However, with thoughtful planning and a balanced approach, it's entirely possible to enjoy these occasions without derailing your progress. The key lies in preparation, mindful choices, and maintaining a positive mindset that allows you to partake in the celebrations while staying true to your goals.

Embracing a Balanced Approach

The first step in planning for special occasions and holidays is to embrace a balanced approach. It's important to recognize that these events are a part of life, and occasional indulgences are not only normal but can also be part of a healthy relationship with food. The goal is not to avoid indulgences entirely but to enjoy them in moderation while maintaining an overall balanced diet.

A balanced approach means giving yourself permission to enjoy your favorite holiday dishes or a special treat at a celebration without guilt. It's about understanding that one meal, or even a few days of indulgence, won't undo all your hard work. The focus should be on the big picture—what you do most of the time matters more than what you do occasionally. This mindset shift allows you to enjoy the moment without the stress of feeling like you've failed. By approaching special occasions with flexibility and mindfulness, you can fully participate in the festivities while making choices that align with your long-term goals.

Planning Ahead for Success

Preparation is key to navigating special occasions and holidays while staying committed to your health goals.

By planning ahead, you can make informed decisions that help you stay on track without feeling deprived.

1. Set Intentions Beforehand:

Before attending an event, take a few moments to set your intentions. Consider what you want to achieve—whether it's enjoying a specific dish, focusing on spending time with loved ones, or simply maintaining your current weight. Setting intentions helps you approach the event with a clear plan, making it easier to make choices that align with your goals.

2. Bring a Healthy Dish:

If you're attending a potluck or holiday gathering, consider bringing a healthy dish that you enjoy. This ensures that there will be at least one option that fits within your dietary preferences. Plus, it's a great way to share delicious, nutritious food with others and introduce them to healthier alternatives.

3. Eat Mindfully Before the Event:

Skipping meals in anticipation of a big event can backfire, leading to overeating once you arrive. Instead, eat a balanced meal or snack before the event, focusing on protein and fiber to keep you satisfied. This can help curb excessive hunger and prevent you from overindulging once the festivities begin.

4. Plan for Indulgences:

If you know there's a particular dish or treat that you want to enjoy, plan for it. Balance your indulgence with lighter choices throughout the day or week. For example, if you're looking forward to a rich dessert, consider having a lighter, vegetable-based meal beforehand. Planning for indulgences allows you to enjoy them without feeling like you've strayed from your healthy habits.

Navigating the Event with Confidence

Once you're at the event, staying mindful and making intentional choices can help you enjoy the occasion while staying committed to your goals.

1. Survey the Spread:

Before filling your plate, take a moment to survey the available options. This allows you to make deliberate choices rather than impulsively grabbing food. Start by filling your plate with vegetables, lean proteins, and other healthier options, leaving room for a small portion of your favorite indulgence.

2. Practice Portion Control:

Portion control is your ally during special occasions. Instead of avoiding certain foods altogether, serve yourself smaller portions. This way, you can enjoy a variety of dishes without overeating. Remember, you can always go back for seconds if you're still hungry, but starting with smaller portions helps prevent overindulgence.

3. Savor Each Bite:

Mindful eating is especially important during special occasions. Take the time to savor each bite, paying attention to the flavors, textures, and aromas. Eating slowly not only enhances your enjoyment of the food but also gives your body time to register fullness, helping you avoid overeating.

4. Focus on the Experience:

Special occasions are about more than just food—they're an opportunity to connect with loved ones and create lasting memories. Shift your focus away from the food and toward the experience. Engage in conversations, participate in activities, and enjoy the company of those around you. By focusing on the social aspects of the event, you're less likely to overeat out of boredom or habit.

Managing Post-Event Mindset

How you handle the days following a special occasion is just as important as how you navigate the event itself. It's common to feel a sense of guilt or regret after indulging, but it's crucial to manage these feelings in a healthy way.

1. Avoid the All-or-Nothing Mentality:

One of the biggest challenges after an indulgent event is the temptation to fall into an all-or-nothing mindset. It's easy to think, "I've already blown my diet, so I might as well keep indulging." Instead, remind yourself that one meal or one day doesn't define your overall progress. Get back to your usual healthy habits at the next meal, and focus on making balanced choices moving forward.

2. Reconnect with Your Routine:

After a special occasion, getting back into your routine can help you regain your focus. Return to your regular meal plan, exercise routine, and hydration habits as soon as possible. This helps you reset and reinforces the healthy habits you've worked hard to establish.

3. Reflect and Learn:

Take a moment to reflect on the event. What went well? What could you have done differently? Use these insights to inform your approach to future events. Each occasion is an opportunity to learn more about yourself and how to maintain balance in your life.

Handling indulgences during special occasions and holidays is a vital skill for sustaining long-term success in your health journey. By embracing a balanced approach, planning ahead, making mindful choices during the event, and managing your post-event mindset, you can enjoy these celebrations without compromising your progress.

6.1 WEEK ONE: STARTING STRONG

WEEK 1	breakfast	snack	lunch	snack	dinner
Monday	OATMEAL WITH BERRIES AND NUTS	APPLE SLICES WITH ALMOND BUTTER	GRILLED CHICKEN SALAD WITH MIXED GREENS AND BALSAMIC VINAIGRETTE	GREEK YOGURT WITH BERRIES	BAKED SALMON WITH STEAMED BROCCOLI AND BROWN RICE
Tuesday	GREEK YOGURT WITH CHIA SEEDS AND HONEY	CARROT STICKS WITH HUMMUS	TURKEY AND AVOCADO WRAP IN WHOLE WHEAT TORTILLA	PROTEIN SHAKE WITH BANANA	GRILLED CHICKEN WITH ASPARAGUS AND SWEET POTATO
Wednesday	VEGGIE OMELETTE WITH SPINACH AND MUSHROOMS	MIXED NUTS AND DRIED FRUIT	QUINOA SALAD WITH BLACK BEANS AND CORN	RICE CAKES WITH ALMOND BUTTER	SPAGHETTI SQUASH WITH MARINARA SAUCE AND GROUND TURKEY
Thursday	SMOOTHIE WITH SPINACH, BANANA, AND PROTEIN POWDER	LOW-FAT CHEESE AND WHOLE GRAIN CRACKERS	LENTIL SOUP WITH WHOLE GRAIN ROLL	TRAIL MIX WITH NUTS AND SEEDS	STUFFED BELL PEPPERS WITH QUINOA AND VEGETABLES
Friday	WHOLE GRAIN TOAST WITH AVOCADO AND EGG	CUCUMBER SLICES WITH TZATZIKI	TUNA SALAD WITH MIXED VEGETABLES	LOW-FAT COTTAGE CHEESE WITH CUCUMBER	GRILLED TILAPIA WITH GREEN BEANS AND QUINOA
Saturday	COTTAGE CHEESE WITH PINEAPPLE AND FLAXSEEDS	CELERY STICKS WITH PEANUT BUTTER	VEGETABLE STIR-FRY WITH TOFU	EDAMAME WITH SEA SALT	VEGETARIAN CHILI WITH BLACK BEANS AND SWEET POTATOES
Sunday	SCRAMBLED TOFU WITH BELL PEPPERS AND ONIONS	HARD-BOILED EGG WITH BABY CARROTS	GRILLED SHRIMP WITH MIXED GREENS AND QUINOA	SMALL FRUIT SALAD	BEEF STIR-FRY WITH BROCCOLI AND BROWN RICE

6.1.1 PREPARING FOR SUCCESS

Preparing for success in your first week of a new meal plan is about more than just following a list of foods; it's about setting the stage for sustainable change. This preparation involves three key areas: organizing your kitchen, planning your grocery shopping, and mentally gearing up for the journey ahead.

Organizing Your Kitchen

Your kitchen is the control center of your meal plan. Start by creating a clean, organized space that invites healthy cooking and mindful eating. Remove any foods that don't align with your goals—processed snacks, sugary treats, and other temptations. This isn't about deprivation; it's about making room for the nourishing foods that will support your success.

Stock your kitchen with the tools you'll need. Make sure you have sharp knives, reliable cookware, and storage containers for meal prep. When your kitchen is ready, you'll find it easier to stick to your plan and enjoy the process of preparing meals.

Planning Your Grocery Shopping

A successful meal plan starts with a well-thought-out shopping trip. Before you head to the store, make a detailed list of the ingredients you'll need for the week.

This list should reflect your meal plan and include everything from main ingredients to healthy snacks. Focus on fresh, whole foods—vegetables, fruits, lean proteins, and whole grains. Shopping the perimeter of the store helps you avoid processed foods that can derail your progress. By planning your shopping in advance, you reduce the risk of impulse purchases and ensure you have everything you need for a week of healthy eating.

Mentally Preparing for the Journey

The mental aspect of starting a new meal plan is just as important as the physical preparation. Set realistic goals for your first week—whether it's following the plan closely, trying new foods, or simply feeling more energized. Visualize your success and remind yourself of why you're embarking on this journey.

Anticipate challenges and plan how you'll handle them. Cravings, social events, and moments of doubt are natural, but with a strong mindset, you can navigate them successfully. Remember, this is a journey, not a sprint. Each step you take, no matter how small, is a step toward lasting change.

As you prepare for week one, focus on creating an environment—both physical and mental—that supports your goals. With your kitchen in order, your shopping planned, and your mindset ready, you're well-equipped to start strong and build momentum for the weeks ahead.

6.1.2 YOUR FIRST WEEK'S MENU:

Your first week on a new meal plan is about building momentum and establishing a routine that feels both manageable and satisfying. This week's menu is designed to guide you day by day, offering balanced meals and snacks that fuel your body and set you up for success. Each day's plan is crafted to provide structure, yet it allows for flexibility, ensuring you can adapt it to your preferences and lifestyle.

Day 1: Setting the Tone

Start your week with a breakfast that combines protein and fiber, giving you sustained energy throughout the morning. A simple yet hearty meal, like eggs with whole-grain toast and a side of fruit, sets a positive tone for the day. Lunch should focus on lean protein and a variety of vegetables—think of a colorful salad topped with grilled chicken or tofu. For dinner, a balanced plate of protein, vegetables, and a small portion of healthy carbs, like quinoa or sweet potato, rounds out the day. Incorporate snacks such as nuts or yogurt to keep hunger at bay and your energy levels stable.

Day 2: Finding Your Rhythm

By day two, you're starting to find your rhythm. Continue with a breakfast that fuels you, such as a smoothie packed with greens, protein powder, and berries. Lunch could be a wrap or sandwich made with whole grains, lean protein, and plenty of veggies. Dinner might feature fish or another protein source, paired with roasted vegetables and a small serving of whole grains. Keep snacks light and nourishing—fruit with a handful of almonds or a small portion of hummus with vegetable sticks.

Day 3: Staying Consistent

Consistency is key, and by day three, you're settling into the plan. Maintain variety in your meals to keep

things interesting. Breakfast might include overnight oats with seeds and fruit. For lunch, a hearty soup or stew with plenty of vegetables and lean protein can be comforting and satisfying. Dinner could be a stir-fry with lean protein, lots of colorful vegetables, and a modest serving of brown rice or another whole grain. Continue to incorporate healthy snacks that keep you feeling full and energized.

Day 4: Midweek Motivation

Midweek can be challenging, but staying motivated is crucial. Start your day with a protein-rich breakfast, such as a veggie omelet. Lunch might be a grain bowl with a mix of greens, protein, and a flavorful dressing. Dinner can be something simple yet satisfying, like grilled chicken or tofu with steamed vegetables and a side salad. Snacks should continue to be balanced— think of a small serving of trail mix or a piece of fruit with nut butter.

Day 5: Building Momentum

As you approach the end of the week, focus on building momentum. A smoothie or a hearty breakfast bowl can kickstart your day. Lunch could be a salad with mixed greens, a variety of vegetables, lean protein, and a light dressing. Dinner might include a lean protein like turkey or beans, paired with roasted or steamed vegetables and a small serving of whole grains. Keep your snacks varied to avoid monotony— perhaps a piece of dark chocolate with nuts or a protein bar that aligns with your nutritional goals.

Day 6: Reflecting and Adjusting

By day six, you may find it helpful to reflect on how the week has gone. Did certain meals work better for you? Use this reflection to adjust your final day. Breakfast might revisit your favorites, while lunch could be a repeat of a meal that left you feeling particularly satisfied. Dinner might be something you've been craving, as long as it fits within your overall plan. Snacks should be tailored to your needs, providing nourishment and satisfaction.

Day 7: Preparing for the Week Ahead

The final day of your first week is about preparing for the next. Start your day with a balanced breakfast that sets a positive tone. For lunch and dinner, consider meals that use up any remaining ingredients from the week, reducing waste and making meal prep easier. Use the day to review what worked well and what didn't, adjusting your plan for the upcoming week. This reflective practice ensures that each week builds on the last, helping you create sustainable habits.

Your first week's menu is designed to support you as you begin this journey. By following this structure and listening to your body's needs, you'll set a strong foundation for the weeks to come. Remember, this is about creating a lifestyle that works for you—one that you can maintain with joy and confidence.

6.1.3 OVERCOMING INITIAL CHALLENGES:

The first week of a new meal plan often brings a mix of excitement and challenges. While you may start with enthusiasm, it's not uncommon to encounter hurdles that test your resolve. These initial challenges are a natural part of the process, and how you handle them can set the tone for your entire journey. By anticipating common obstacles and having strategies in place to overcome them, you can stay on track and build momentum for the weeks ahead.

Managing Cravings and Hunger

One of the most common challenges in the first week is dealing with cravings and unexpected hunger. Your body is adjusting to a new way of eating, and it might resist by urging you to reach for familiar comfort foods. The key to overcoming this is preparation and mindfulness.

Ensure that your meals and snacks are balanced with enough protein, fiber, and healthy fats, which help keep you full and satisfied. If a craving hits, pause and ask yourself whether you're truly hungry or if it's an emotional response. Sometimes, a glass of water or a short walk can help you determine whether you need to eat or if the craving will pass on its own. When hunger is genuine, reach for a healthy, pre-planned snack to stay on track.

Dealing with Fatigue

As your body adapts to a new diet, especially one that might be lower in calories or different in nutrient composition, you might experience fatigue. This is particularly true if you're also starting a new exercise routine. Fatigue can be discouraging, but it's important to remember that it's usually temporary.

Combat fatigue by ensuring you're getting enough sleep, staying hydrated, and fueling your body with nutrient-dense foods. Don't skip meals or severely restrict your intake—doing so can lead to energy crashes and make it harder to stick to your plan. Listen to your body's needs, and if necessary, adjust your activity level during this adjustment period. The goal is to find a sustainable balance that allows you to feel energized and motivated.

Navigating Social Situations

Social events can be challenging, especially when they involve food that's not part of your plan. Whether it's a dinner with friends or a work gathering, it's easy to feel pressured to indulge or stray from your meal plan. The best strategy is to plan ahead. If possible, eat a healthy snack before the event to avoid arriving hungry. At the event, focus on portion control and choose the healthiest options available. Don't hesitate to bring your own dish if appropriate. Most importantly, give yourself permission to enjoy the occasion without guilt—remember, one meal won't derail your progress, but how you respond afterward is key.

Staying Motivated

The first week can be mentally challenging as you adjust to new habits and resist old ones. It's important to stay connected to your "why"—the reasons you embarked on this journey in the first place. Visualize your goals and remind yourself of the benefits you're working toward, whether it's improved health, increased energy, or greater self-confidence.

If you find your motivation waning, consider tracking your progress, no matter how small. Celebrate the victories, like sticking to your plan for a day or trying a new healthy recipe. These small wins build confidence and reinforce your commitment.

Overcoming the initial challenges of the first week is about preparation, mindfulness, and staying connected to your goals. By managing cravings, dealing with fatigue, navigating social situations, and maintaining your motivation, you can stay on track and lay a strong foundation for the weeks to come. Remember, each challenge you face and overcome makes you stronger and more resilient, bringing you one step closer to long-term success.

6.2 WEEK TWO: BUILDING MOMENTUM

WEEK 1	breakfast	snack	lunch	snack	dinner
Monday	OATMEAL WITH BERRIES AND NUTS	APPLE SLICES WITH ALMOND BUTTER	GRILLED CHICKEN SALAD WITH MIXED GREENS AND BALSAMIC VINAIGRETTE	GREEK YOGURT WITH BERRIES	BAKED SALMON WITH STEAMED BROCCOLI AND BROWN RICE
Tuesday	GREEK YOGURT WITH CHIA SEEDS AND HONEY	CARROT STICKS WITH HUMMUS	TURKEY AND AVOCADO WRAP IN WHOLE WHEAT TORTILLA	PROTEIN SHAKE WITH BANANA	GRILLED CHICKEN WITH ASPARAGUS AND SWEET POTATO
Wednesday	VEGGIE OMELETTE WITH SPINACH AND MUSHROOMS	MIXED NUTS AND DRIED FRUIT	QUINOA SALAD WITH BLACK BEANS AND CORN	RICE CAKES WITH ALMOND BUTTER	SPAGHETTI SQUASH WITH MARINARA SAUCE AND GROUND TURKEY
Thursday	SMOOTHIE WITH SPINACH, BANANA, AND PROTEIN POWDER	LOW-FAT CHEESE AND WHOLE GRAIN CRACKERS	LENTIL SOUP WITH WHOLE GRAIN ROLL	TRAIL MIX WITH NUTS AND SEEDS	STUFFED BELL PEPPERS WITH QUINOA AND VEGETABLES
Friday	WHOLE GRAIN TOAST WITH AVOCADO AND EGG	CUCUMBER SLICES WITH TZATZIKI	TUNA SALAD WITH MIXED VEGETABLES	LOW-FAT COTTAGE CHEESE WITH CUCUMBER	GRILLED TILAPIA WITH GREEN BEANS AND QUINOA
Saturday	COTTAGE CHEESE WITH PINEAPPLE AND FLAXSEEDS	CELERY STICKS WITH PEANUT BUTTER	VEGETABLE STIR-FRY WITH TOFU	EDAMAME WITH SEA SALT	VEGETARIAN CHILI WITH BLACK BEANS AND SWEET POTATOES
Sunday	SCRAMBLED TOFU WITH BELL PEPPERS AND ONIONS	HARD-BOILED EGG WITH BABY CARROTS	GRILLED SHRIMP WITH MIXED GREENS AND QUINOA	SMALL FRUIT SALAD	BEEF STIR-FRY WITH BROCCOLI AND BROWN RICE

6.2.1 ADJUSTING TO YOUR NEW ROUTINE:

As you transition into Week Two of your meal plan, the focus shifts from establishing routines to fine-tuning them. The first week was about laying the groundwork, but now it's time to listen to your body and make adjustments that ensure your plan is not only sustainable but also enjoyable. This process of tweaking and adapting is crucial for building momentum and setting yourself up for long-term success.

Listening to Your Body

Your body is an incredible source of feedback, and during the first week, it likely provided some important signals. You may have experienced changes in energy levels, hunger patterns, or even cravings. These cues are essential as they help you understand how well your current meal plan is serving you.

If you noticed consistent hunger between meals, it might be a sign that you need to increase the volume of your meals, particularly by adding more fiber or lean protein. On the other hand, if you felt overly full or sluggish after certain meals, consider adjusting portion sizes or the balance of macronutrients. The goal is to create a plan that fuels you adequately throughout the day, keeping you energized and satisfied without overeating.

Tweaking Your Meal Plan

Adjustments to your meal plan should be thoughtful and deliberate. Start by reflecting on what worked well in Week One and what didn't. If you found certain meals particularly enjoyable and satisfying, make them a regular part of your rotation. If there were meals that didn't appeal to you or left you feeling unsatisfied, it's time to modify them or replace them with alternatives that better suit your taste and nutritional needs.

Consider also the practical aspects of your plan. Was meal *PREPARATION TIME*-consuming or stressful? If so, look for ways to streamline the process in Week Two. This might involve prepping ingredients in bulk, choosing simpler recipes, or even incorporating more leftovers into your meal planning. The easier and more enjoyable the process, the more likely you are to stick with it.

Building Flexibility

As you adjust your routine, it's important to build in flexibility. Life is unpredictable, and there will be days when things don't go according to plan. Developing a mindset that allows for flexibility—without guilt—can help you navigate these situations without feeling derailed. This might mean having a few go-to quick meals on hand for busy days or learning how to make healthy choices when dining out.

Remember, the adjustments you make in Week Two are not just about optimizing your meal plan for immediate results, but about creating a sustainable routine that you can maintain over time. This is your opportunity to personalize the plan to fit your lifestyle and preferences, ensuring that it continues to support your goals as you move forward.

By the end of Week Two, you'll have a clearer understanding of what works best for you, laying a solid foundation for the weeks to come. Embrace this period of adjustment as a natural part of your journey, and take pride in the progress you're making toward a healthier, more balanced life.

6.2.2 FOCUSED NUTRITION:

As you move into Week Two of your meal plan, the focus shifts to enhancing the variety in your meals while maintaining balanced nutrition. This is a crucial step in building momentum, as incorporating a diverse range of foods not only keeps your meals exciting but also ensures you're getting a broad spectrum of nutrients that support your overall health.

Expanding Your Food Choices

In the first week, you likely stuck to a set of familiar, straightforward meals as you established your routine. Now, it's time to expand your repertoire. Introducing new foods into your diet can help prevent boredom and keep your palate engaged, making it easier to stick with your plan long-term. Variety also plays a key role in ensuring that your body receives all the essential vitamins, minerals, and other nutrients it needs.

Start by incorporating a wider range of vegetables and fruits into your meals. Each color of produce brings different nutrients to the table—such as the antioxidants in berries, the beta-carotene in carrots, or the vitamin C in citrus fruits. Aim to create colorful plates that not only look appealing but also provide a variety of health benefits.

Beyond fruits and vegetables, consider exploring different protein sources. If you've been relying on chicken and fish, try adding plant-based options like lentils, beans, or tofu into your meals. These not only diversify your protein intake but also introduce beneficial fiber and phytonutrients into your diet.

Balancing Nutrients

While adding variety, it's important to keep your meals balanced. Each meal should ideally include a mix of protein, healthy fats, and complex carbohydrates. This balance helps maintain stable energy levels, supports muscle maintenance, and keeps you feeling satisfied throughout the day.

For example, if you're adding a new grain like quinoa to your diet, balance it with a protein source such as grilled fish or chickpeas, and include a side of mixed vegetables. Similarly, when trying out a new vegetable, pair it with a familiar protein and a healthy fat like avocado or olive oil. This approach ensures that while your meals are varied, they're also meeting your nutritional needs.

Mindful Exploration

As you introduce more variety, remain mindful of how these changes affect your body. Pay attention to how different foods make you feel, both physically and mentally. Do they provide sustained energy? Do they leave you feeling full and satisfied? Use this feedback to continue refining your meal plan, focusing on foods that not only nourish your body but also bring you joy.

By embracing a wider range of foods while maintaining nutritional balance, you'll make your meal plan more enjoyable and sustainable. This variety not only fuels your body with the essential nutrients it needs but also helps you build a positive, flexible relationship with food—one that will support you well beyond these five weeks.

6.2.3 STAYING MOTIVATED

As you move into Week Two, maintaining your motivation is crucial for building momentum. The initial excitement of starting something new might begin to wane, but this is the time to dig deep and reinforce your commitment. Staying motivated doesn't just happen; it requires intentional strategies that keep your energy high and your focus sharp.

Connecting with Your "Why"

At the core of sustained motivation is a clear understanding of why you started this journey in the first place. Take a few moments each day to reconnect with your personal reasons for embarking on this meal plan. Whether it's improving your health, gaining more energy, or feeling more confident in your body, keeping your "why" at the forefront of your mind can serve as a powerful motivator when challenges arise.

Consider writing down your goals and placing them somewhere visible—on the fridge, next to your bed, or even as a reminder on your phone. These visual cues can help you stay focused and motivated, especially on days when your resolve might feel tested.

Celebrating Small Wins

One of the most effective ways to maintain motivation is to celebrate your progress, no matter how small. Each healthy meal, every workout completed, and even the decision to stick to your plan in the face of temptation is a victory worth acknowledging. These small wins build momentum and reinforce positive behavior.

At the end of each day, take a moment to reflect on what you did well. Did you try a new vegetable? Did you resist the urge to snack late at night? These are all steps in the right direction. By focusing on what you've accomplished, rather than what you have yet to do, you keep your motivation high and your outlook positive.

Staying Energized

Maintaining physical energy is just as important as staying mentally motivated. Ensure that your meals are balanced and nourishing, providing the energy you need to stay active and focused throughout the day. Incorporate regular physical activity into your routine, even if it's just a brisk walk or a quick stretch. Exercise not only boosts your energy levels but also releases endorphins, which enhance your mood and motivation.

Rest is equally important. Make sure you're getting enough sleep each night to allow your body to recover and recharge. A well-rested body is more resilient and better equipped to handle the challenges of a new routine.

Seeking Support

Remember, you don't have to do this alone. Reach out to friends, family, or a support group for encouragement. Sharing your journey with others who understand your goals can provide a sense of community and accountability. Don't hesitate to ask for support when you need it—whether it's a motivational pep talk, help with meal prep, or simply someone to listen.

Week Two is about building on the foundation you set in the first week, and staying motivated is key to that progress. By connecting with your "why," celebrating small wins, staying energized, and seeking support, you can keep your motivation strong and your energy high. This is the time to push through any dips in enthusiasm and continue moving forward, knowing that each day brings you closer to your long-term goals.

6.3 WEEK THREE: FINDING YOUR RHYTHM

WEEK 3	breakfast	snack	lunch	snack	dinner
Monday	EGG WHITE OMELETTE WITH SPINACH AND TOMATOES	CELERY STICKS WITH HUMMUS	CHICKEN SALAD WITH AVOCADO AND MIXED GREENS	APPLE SLICES WITH PEANUT BUTTER	GRILLED CHICKEN BREAST WITH QUINOA AND BROCCOLI
Tuesday	SMOOTHIE WITH MANGO, GREEK YOGURT, AND SPINACH	LOW-FAT STRING CHEESE WITH GRAPES	GRILLED SHRIMP WITH COUSCOUS AND SPINACH	COTTAGE CHEESE WITH CUCUMBER SLICES	BEEF STIR-FRY WITH MIXED VEGETABLES AND BROWN RICE
Wednesday	WHOLE GRAIN TOAST WITH PEANUT BUTTER AND BANANA	ALMOND BUTTER ON WHOLE GRAIN CRACKERS	TURKEY WRAP WITH WHOLE GRAIN TORTILLA AND LETTUCE	RICE CAKES WITH AVOCADO AND TOMATO	BAKED TILAPIA WITH WILD RICE AND STEAMED CARROTS
Thursday	OATMEAL WITH ALMOND BUTTER AND APPLE SLICES	CARROT STICKS WITH YOGURT DIP	MEDITERRANEAN QUINOA SALAD WITH CHICKPEAS	HARD-BOILED EGG WITH CELERY STICKS	VEGETARIAN CHILI WITH BLACK BEANS AND CORN
Friday	VEGGIE SCRAMBLE WITH ZUCCHINI AND MUSHROOMS	MIXED NUTS WITH DRIED APRICOTS	VEGETABLE STIR-FRY WITH TOFU AND BROWN RICE	BANANA SLICES WITH ALMOND BUTTER	GRILLED TURKEY BURGER WITH WHOLE GRAIN BUN AND SALAD
Saturday	COTTAGE CHEESE WITH PEACHES AND WALNUTS	BELL PEPPER STRIPS WITH SALSA	GRILLED SALMON WITH ASPARAGUS AND SWEET POTATO	LOW-FAT YOGURT WITH MIXED BERRIES	SPAGHETTI SQUASH WITH MARINARA SAUCE AND GROUND TURKEY
Sunday	AVOCADO SMOOTHIE WITH KALE AND PINEAPPLE	GREEK YOGURT WITH HONEY AND CINNAMON	CHICKEN CAESAR WRAP WITH ROMAINE AND PARMESAN	SMOOTHIE WITH SPINACH, PINEAPPLE, AND PROTEIN POWDER	VEGETABLE SOUP WITH LENTILS AND WHOLE GRAIN ROLL

6.3.1 ESTABLISHING CONSISTENT HABITS

As you enter Week Three, the focus shifts toward establishing consistent habits that will carry you through not just the next few weeks, but long after your meal plan ends. By now, you've gained momentum and have a sense of what works best for you. The key is to solidify these routines, making them second nature, so that healthy eating becomes a seamless part of your life.

Mastering Meal Prep

Meal prepping is one of the most effective strategies for maintaining consistency in your eating habits. By planning and preparing your meals in advance, you reduce the likelihood of making impulsive, less healthy food choices. It also saves time during busy weekdays, allowing you to stick to your plan with minimal stress. To solidify your meal prep routine, start by choosing a specific day each week to plan, shop, and prepare your meals. This could be Sunday afternoon or another time that fits your schedule. Dedicate a few hours to cooking, portioning, and storing your meals for the week. Focus on recipes that are easy to prepare in bulk and that hold up well in the fridge or freezer. Having a variety of pre-prepared meals on hand ensures that you always have a healthy option available, even on your busiest days.

Creating Sustainable Eating Habits

Establishing consistent habits goes beyond meal prep; it's about creating a sustainable approach to eating that feels natural and enjoyable. This means finding a balance that allows you to nourish your body without feeling deprived. Pay attention to how different foods make you feel and adjust your choices accordingly. If a particular routine or meal isn't working for you, don't be afraid to make changes. The goal is to develop habits that you can maintain for the long term. Part of this process involves listening to your body's hunger and fullness cues. Eating when you're hungry and stopping when you're satisfied—not stuffed—helps you build a positive relationship with food. This mindful approach to eating encourages you to tune in to your body's needs and make choices that support your health and well-being.

Building Flexibility into Your Routine

While consistency is important, it's also crucial to remain flexible. Life is unpredictable, and there will be times when your routine is disrupted. The ability to adapt without feeling like you've failed is key to maintaining your habits over time. If something unexpected comes up—like a spontaneous dinner out or a change in your schedule—focus on making the best choices available and getting back to your routine as soon as possible.

Week Three is about finding your rhythm and establishing habits that will support your goals long-term. By mastering meal prep, creating sustainable eating habits, and building flexibility into your routine, you lay the foundation for lasting success. These habits, once established, will make healthy eating feel effortless, allowing you to enjoy the benefits of your hard work for years to come.

6.3.2 TWEAKING YOUR PLAN

By Week Three, you've had time to settle into your meal plan and begin to understand what works best for you. This is the perfect moment to start customizing the plan to better align with your preferences, lifestyle, and nutritional needs. The process of tweaking your plan is about making adjustments that not only make the diet more enjoyable but also more sustainable in the long run.

Listening to Your Preferences

As you've followed the meal plan over the past two weeks, you've likely discovered which meals and ingredients you enjoy most and which ones you're less enthusiastic about. Use this insight to refine your plan. If there's a particular food or meal that you find yourself looking forward to, consider incorporating it more frequently. Conversely, if there's something that you find difficult to stick with, think about alternatives that could serve the same nutritional purpose but better suit your tastes.

Customization is key to ensuring that the meal plan feels like it's tailored to you, rather than something you're forcing yourself to follow. This could mean swapping out certain proteins, experimenting with different vegetables, or adjusting portion sizes to better fit your hunger levels. The goal is to create a plan that you enjoy and that supports your health, making it easier to maintain over time.

Adapting to Your Lifestyle

Everyone's lifestyle is different, and a meal plan should accommodate your unique schedule and responsibilities. By Week Three, you've had enough experience to know which aspects of the plan fit seamlessly into your daily routine and which ones might need tweaking.

For instance, if you find that preparing elaborate meals every evening is too time-consuming, consider simplifying your dinners with quicker, easier recipes. If you're always on the go during the day, focus on portable, easy-to-eat options for lunches and snacks. The idea is to adapt the plan so that it works with your life, not against it.

Adjusting for Long-Term Sustainability

Sustainability is the cornerstone of any successful meal plan. As you customize your plan, keep long-term adherence in mind. The tweaks you make now should not only make the plan more enjoyable but also more realistic to follow indefinitely.

If you've been strict with certain restrictions or portions, now might be the time to ease up slightly, as long as it doesn't compromise your overall goals. Flexibility is crucial—life will always present unexpected challenges, and your plan should be robust enough to handle them without causing stress or a sense of failure.

Tweaking your meal plan in Week Three is about finding the balance between enjoyment and effectiveness. By listening to your preferences, adapting the plan to fit your lifestyle, and making adjustments that support long-term sustainability, you transform the meal plan from a short-term solution into a lasting part of your life. This personalization not only makes the diet more enjoyable but also empowers you to take ownership of your health journey.

6.3.3 PREPARING FOR LONG-TERM SUCCESS

By the time you reach Week Three, you're no longer just following a meal plan—you're starting to integrate it into your life. This is a pivotal moment to begin focusing on the mindset shifts that will help you sustain your progress long after the five weeks are over. Preparing for long-term success involves embracing a new way of thinking about food, health, and your personal goals.

Shifting from Short-Term to Long-Term Thinking

One of the most significant mindset shifts is moving away from the idea of a diet as a temporary fix. Instead, begin to view your current efforts as the foundation of a lasting lifestyle. The habits you're developing now—mindful eating, balanced nutrition, regular meal prep—are not just for these five weeks but for a lifetime.

To cultivate this mindset, reflect on your journey so far and recognize the positive changes you've made. Perhaps you're feeling more energetic, your clothes fit better, or you've developed a new appreciation for healthy foods. These are not just short-term wins but indicators of the long-term benefits that will come from maintaining these habits. By focusing on the sustainability of your actions, you shift your goal from simply reaching a number on the scale to living a healthier, more balanced life.

Embracing Flexibility and Balance

Another crucial mindset shift is embracing flexibility. Life is unpredictable, and strict adherence to any plan can lead to frustration and burnout. Understanding that it's okay to adjust your approach as circumstances change is key to long-term success.

Instead of aiming for perfection, strive for balance. This might mean allowing yourself occasional indulgences without guilt, knowing that what matters most is consistency over time. By adopting a flexible, balanced approach, you reduce the pressure on yourself and create a more sustainable relationship with food.

Cultivating Self-Compassion

Self-compassion is another essential element of long-term success. There will be days when you deviate from your plan, face setbacks, or feel less motivated. How you respond to these moments is critical. Rather than falling into a cycle of self-criticism, practice kindness toward yourself. Acknowledge that setbacks are a natural part of any journey and use them as opportunities to learn and grow.

By cultivating self-compassion, you build resilience. This resilience helps you bounce back from challenges and maintain your progress over the long term. It also encourages a more positive and empowering relationship with yourself, which is essential for sustaining any healthy lifestyle change.

As you progress through Week Three, focus on the mindset shifts that will support your long-term success. By moving from short-term to long-term thinking, embracing flexibility, and cultivating self-compassion, you're not just following a meal plan—you're creating a sustainable, balanced lifestyle. These mindset shifts will carry you beyond the five-week plan, helping you maintain your progress and continue growing in your health journey.

6.4 WEEK FOUR: REFINING YOUR CHOICES

WEEK 4	breakfast	snack	lunch	snack	dinner
Monday	PROTEIN SMOOTHIE WITH SPINACH, BANANA, AND CHIA SEEDS	SLICED CUCUMBERS WITH HUMMUS	GRILLED CHICKEN SALAD WITH MIXED GREENS AND BALSAMIC VINAIGRETTE	MIXED NUTS WITH DRIED CHERRIES	BAKED SALMON WITH ASPARAGUS AND QUINOA
Tuesday	EGG WHITE SCRAMBLE WITH BELL PEPPERS AND ONIONS	APPLE SLICES WITH PEANUT BUTTER	QUINOA BOWL WITH BLACK BEANS, CORN, AND AVOCADO	LOW-FAT COTTAGE CHEESE WITH PINEAPPLE	CHICKEN STIR-FRY WITH BROCCOLI AND BROWN RICE
Wednesday	OVERNIGHT OATS WITH BLUEBERRIES AND ALMONDS	GREEK YOGURT WITH FLAXSEEDS	VEGETABLE STIR-FRY WITH SHRIMP AND BROWN RICE	CELERY STICKS WITH PEANUT BUTTER	SPAGHETTI SQUASH WITH TURKEY MEATBALLS
Thursday	WHOLE GRAIN BAGEL WITH AVOCADO AND TOMATO	RAW ALMONDS AND DRIED APRICOTS	TUNA SALAD WITH WHOLE GRAIN CRACKERS	PROTEIN SHAKE WITH BANANA	GRILLED STEAK WITH SWEET POTATO AND GREEN BEANS
Friday	GREEK YOGURT PARFAIT WITH STRAWBERRIES AND GRANOLA	CARROT STICKS WITH GUACAMOLE	VEGAN CHILI WITH LENTILS AND SWEET POTATO	LOW-FAT CHEESE WITH WHOLE GRAIN CRACKERS	VEGETARIAN STUFFED PEPPERS WITH QUINOA AND BLACK BEANS
Saturday	OATMEAL WITH WALNUTS AND DRIED CRANBERRIES	BELL PEPPER SLICES WITH COTTAGE CHEESE	GRILLED TURKEY SANDWICH WITH LETTUCE AND TOMATO	HUMMUS WITH BABY CARROTS	SHRIMP FAJITAS WITH WHOLE WHEAT TORTILLAS
Sunday	VEGGIE OMELETTE WITH FETA AND SPINACH	PROTEIN BAR WITH DARK CHOCOLATE	SPINACH AND FETA WRAP WITH WHOLE GRAIN TORTILLA	SMOOTHIE WITH SPINACH, APPLE, AND GINGER	BAKED CHICKEN BREAST WITH BRUSSELS SPROUTS AND WILD RICE

6.4.1 ENHANCING YOUR MEAL PREP

By Week Four, you've likely established a solid meal prep routine that helps you stay on track with your plan. Now, it's time to take your meal prep skills to the next level. Advanced meal prep techniques can save you even more time and add variety to your diet, keeping your meals both convenient and exciting. Enhancing these skills ensures that your meal prep routine not only supports your current goals but also becomes a sustainable part of your lifestyle.

Batch Cooking with Variety

One of the most effective advanced meal prep techniques is batch cooking with a focus on variety. Instead of preparing the same meal for every day of the week, try cooking larger quantities of different components that can be mixed and matched throughout the week. For example, roast a variety of vegetables, cook a few different types of proteins, and prepare grains like quinoa or brown rice. This approach allows you to assemble different meals each day, keeping your diet varied and your palate engaged. By having a range of options ready, you can easily customize your meals based on your mood, cravings, or nutritional needs. This flexibility not only saves time but also reduces the monotony that can sometimes come with meal prep.

Freezing for Future Meals

Another advanced technique is incorporating freezing into your meal prep routine. Freezing meals or components of meals can be a game-changer, especially for those days when you're too busy to cook. Consider doubling recipes and freezing half for later use. Soups, stews, casseroles, and even pre-cooked proteins can be stored in the freezer and quickly reheated when needed.

Proper labeling is key—make sure to note the date and contents on each container. This ensures you're always aware of what's available and can plan accordingly. Freezing meals not only extends the life of your prep work but also provides a safety net for weeks when life gets particularly hectic.

Maximizing Efficiency with Kitchen Tools

To enhance your meal prep efficiency, consider investing in kitchen tools that streamline the process. Appliances like slow cookers, pressure cookers, and food processors can significantly reduce the time and effort required to prepare large quantities of food. These tools allow you to focus on other tasks while your meals cook, making the prep process less hands-on and more manageable.

Additionally, consider using storage containers that are stackable and easy to organize. This helps keep your fridge and freezer tidy and ensures you can quickly find what you need. A well-organized kitchen can make meal prep faster and more enjoyable, encouraging you to stick with it.

Enhancing your meal prep skills in Week Four is about maximizing efficiency and ensuring variety in your diet. By batch cooking with variety, incorporating freezing into your routine, and utilizing time-saving kitchen tools, you can refine your meal prep process to better support your goals. These advanced techniques not only save time but also make it easier to maintain a balanced, nutritious diet over the long term, ensuring your meal prep routine is both sustainable and enjoyable.

6.4.2 EXPLORING NEW RECIPES

As you approach Week Four, you've likely settled into a comfortable routine with your meals. However, even the most balanced and nutritious plan can start to feel repetitive over time. To keep your meals exciting and prevent diet fatigue, it's essential to introduce new recipes that align with your nutritional goals while bringing fresh flavors and experiences to your table. This exploration not only invigorates your palate but also reinforces your commitment to maintaining a healthy lifestyle.

The Benefits of Variety

Incorporating new recipes into your meal plan offers numerous benefits beyond just keeping things interesting. Variety in your diet ensures you're getting a broader range of nutrients, as different foods provide different vitamins, minerals, and other essential nutrients. This diversity supports overall health and can help prevent deficiencies that might arise from eating the same foods repeatedly.

Exploring new recipes also stimulates your creativity in the kitchen. Trying out different cuisines, cooking techniques, and ingredients can make meal preparation more enjoyable and less of a chore. When you're excited about what you're cooking, you're more

likely to stick with your meal plan and continue making healthy choices.

Finding Inspiration

To introduce new recipes into your routine, start by seeking inspiration from various sources. Cookbooks, food blogs, and social media platforms like Instagram and Pinterest are treasure troves of ideas. Look for recipes that feature ingredients you enjoy but prepare them in new and inventive ways. Don't hesitate to explore cuisines you're less familiar with—whether it's a vibrant Thai curry, a comforting Italian soup, or a fresh Mediterranean salad, the world of food offers endless possibilities.

As you explore, consider your current meal plan and look for recipes that complement it. If you've been enjoying grilled chicken, for example, you might try a recipe that uses chicken in a different context, such as a stir-fry with Asian vegetables or a baked dish with a flavorful spice rub. These variations keep your meals fresh without straying too far from the foods you know work well for you.

Experimenting with Ingredients

Introducing new ingredients is another way to keep your meals exciting. If you've been relying on the same vegetables or grains, consider experimenting with others that offer different textures and flavors. For example, swap out your usual brown rice for farro or quinoa, or try roasting root vegetables like parsnips or beets instead of your standard potatoes and carrots.

These small changes can make a significant difference in your meal experience, adding complexity and depth to your dishes. They also keep your taste buds engaged, reducing the temptation to stray from your plan due to boredom.

Exploring new recipes in Week Four is an opportunity to refresh your meal plan and maintain your enthusiasm for healthy eating. By introducing variety through new dishes and ingredients, you prevent diet fatigue and ensure that your meals continue to be a source of enjoyment and nourishment. This approach not only keeps you motivated but also supports a well-rounded, sustainable diet that you'll be eager to continue beyond the five-week plan.

6.4.3 EVALUATING YOUR PROGRESS

As you near the end of Week Four, it's time to take a step back and reflect on your journey so far. Evaluating your progress is not just about assessing results on the scale but about considering how you feel, how well you've integrated your new habits, and where you might need to make adjustments. This reflection is a powerful tool to ensure that you're not only achieving your goals but also setting the stage for long-term success.

Reflecting on Physical and Emotional Changes

Start by considering the physical changes you've noticed since beginning the meal plan. Have you experienced weight loss, increased energy levels, or improvements in your overall health? These tangible results are important markers of progress, but they're not the only ones that matter. Equally significant are the emotional and psychological changes you've undergone. Reflect on your relationship with food—do you feel more in control, more mindful, and less prone to emotional eating? These shifts are crucial indicators of your journey's success and are often the foundation for sustainable, long-term change.

Assessing Habit Formation

By Week Four, certain habits should be becoming second nature. Reflect on the routines you've established around meal prepping, mindful eating, and physical activity. Are these habits feeling more natural and less like a chore? If certain aspects of your plan are still challenging, now is the time to evaluate why that might be. Perhaps you need to simplify your meal prep process, find more enjoyable forms of exercise, or adjust your eating schedule to better fit your lifestyle. The key is to identify what's working and what isn't, and to make thoughtful adjustments that will enhance your results.

Making Strategic Adjustments

Based on your reflection, consider what adjustments might help you enhance your progress. This could involve tweaking your meal plan to better suit your tastes and nutritional needs, increasing or varying your physical activity, or implementing new strategies to stay motivated. These adjustments don't have to be drastic—often, small, incremental changes can make a significant difference.

For example, if you've noticed that your energy levels dip in the afternoon, consider adding a protein-rich snack to your routine. If you're feeling bored with your workouts, try a new class or activity to reignite your enthusiasm. The goal of these adjustments is to keep your plan dynamic and responsive to your evolving needs, ensuring that you continue to make progress without feeling stagnant.

Evaluating your progress in Week Four is a crucial step in refining your choices and enhancing your results. By reflecting on both the physical and emotional changes you've experienced, assessing the habits you've formed, and making strategic adjustments, you set yourself up for continued success. This process of reflection and adjustment ensures that your journey remains positive, sustainable, and aligned with your long-term goals, carrying you confidently into the final week and beyond.

6.5 WEEK FIVE: CEMENTING YOUR NEW LIFESTYLE

WEEK 5	breakfast	snack	lunch	snack	dinner
Monday	SPINACH AND MUSHROOM OMELETTE WITH FETA CHEESE	CELERY STICKS WITH ALMOND BUTTER	GRILLED CHICKEN CAESAR SALAD WITH KALE AND PARMESAN	RICE CAKES WITH PEANUT BUTTER AND BANANA	GRILLED SALMON WITH ASPARAGUS AND SWEET POTATO
Tuesday	GREEK YOGURT WITH MIXED BERRIES AND ALMONDS	LOW-FAT STRING CHEESE WITH APPLE SLICES	QUINOA SALAD WITH CHICKPEAS, CUCUMBERS, AND TOMATOES	GREEK YOGURT WITH GRANOLA	CHICKEN BREAST WITH QUINOA AND STEAMED BROCCOLI
Wednesday	OVERNIGHT OATS WITH CHIA SEEDS AND BANANA	GREEK YOGURT WITH HONEY AND WALNUTS	TURKEY SANDWICH WITH WHOLE GRAIN BREAD AND AVOCADO	SLICED BELL PEPPERS WITH RANCH DRESSING	SPAGHETTI SQUASH WITH MARINARA AND GROUND TURKEY
Thursday	WHOLE GRAIN PANCAKES WITH BLUEBERRIES AND MAPLE SYRUP	BABY CARROTS WITH HUMMUS	SHRIMP AND VEGETABLE STIR-FRY WITH BROWN RICE	COTTAGE CHEESE WITH PINEAPPLE	BAKED COD WITH WILD RICE AND GREEN BEANS
Friday	SMOOTHIE WITH KALE, PINEAPPLE, AND PROTEIN POWDER	MIXED NUTS WITH DRIED CRANBERRIES	LENTIL SOUP WITH SPINACH AND WHOLE GRAIN ROLL	HUMMUS WITH WHOLE GRAIN CRACKERS	VEGETABLE STIR-FRY WITH TOFU AND BROWN RICE
Saturday	AVOCADO TOAST WITH POACHED EGG AND TOMATO	COTTAGE CHEESE WITH PEACHES	GRILLED FISH TACOS WITH CABBAGE SLAW	APPLE SLICES WITH ALMOND BUTTER	TURKEY MEATLOAF WITH MASHED CAULIFLOWER AND PEAS
Sunday	SCRAMBLED EGGS WITH PEPPERS AND ONIONS	PROTEIN SHAKE WITH SPINACH AND BANANA	VEGETARIAN CHILI WITH BROWN RICE	LOW-FAT CHEESE WITH WHOLE GRAIN CRACKERS	GRILLED SHRIMP WITH COUSCOUS AND STEAMED SPINACH

6.5.1 FINAL PUSH FOR RESULTS

As you enter the final week of your five-week journey, the focus shifts to making a strong push to maximize your results. This last phase is not just about reinforcing the habits you've built, but also about fine-tuning your approach to ensure you achieve the best possible outcomes. The strategies you employ in these final days can significantly impact both your weight loss and overall health improvements, setting the stage for a smooth transition into a sustainable, long-term lifestyle.

Intensifying Your Focus

In this final week, it's crucial to intensify your focus on the elements of your plan that have yielded the best results. Reflect on what has worked particularly well for you—whether it's a specific type of exercise, a particular meal structure, or the timing of your meals. Double down on these strategies, making sure to maintain consistency and avoid any distractions that could derail your progress.

Now is also the time to pay close attention to portion control. While you don't want to drastically cut calories, being mindful of portion sizes can help you shed those last few pounds. Focus on nutrient-dense foods that provide satiety without excessive calories, ensuring that every bite counts towards your goals.

Optimizing Your Workouts

To maximize your results, consider ramping up your physical activity in this final week. If you've been following a regular exercise routine, see if you can push a bit harder—whether that means adding an extra workout, increasing the intensity, or incorporating different forms of exercise that challenge your body in new ways.

High-intensity interval training (HIIT), strength training, and cardio are all excellent ways to boost your calorie burn and improve muscle tone. Even small changes, like adding an extra set of reps or increasing the weight you're lifting, can make a significant difference. The goal is to finish the week feeling strong, energized, and accomplished.

Prioritizing Rest and Recovery

While it's important to push hard in this final week, it's equally important to prioritize rest and recovery. Your body needs time to repair and rebuild, especially if you've increased the intensity of your workouts. Make sure you're getting enough sleep each night, as sleep plays a crucial role in weight loss, muscle recovery, and overall health.

Incorporating stress-reducing practices like meditation, deep breathing, or gentle yoga can also help you stay balanced and focused. Remember, stress can negatively impact your progress by affecting your hormones and leading to cravings or overeating. Keeping stress in check will help you maintain a positive mindset and stay on track.

Staying Hydrated and Mindful

Hydration is another key factor in maximizing your results. Drinking plenty of water helps flush out toxins, supports digestion, and can even boost your metabolism. Aim to stay well-hydrated throughout the day, particularly before meals, to help control appetite and prevent overeating.

Mindfulness continues to play a critical role in your success. As you move through this final week, remain conscious of your choices, savor your meals, and celebrate your progress. By staying present and focused, you reinforce the healthy habits that will carry you into the next phase of your journey.

The final week of your meal plan is about making a strong push for the best possible results. By intensifying your focus, optimizing your workouts, prioritizing rest, and staying mindful, you set yourself up for success. These strategies will not only help you maximize your weight loss and health improvements but also ensure that you finish the plan feeling empowered and ready to maintain your new lifestyle. As you close out this chapter, remember that the habits and strategies you've developed are the foundation for ongoing health and well-being.

6.5.2 PREPARING FOR LIFE AFTER THE MEAL

As you reach the final stretch of your five-week meal plan, the focus naturally shifts toward life beyond this structured period. Transitioning from a defined meal plan to a sustainable, long-term lifestyle is a crucial step in ensuring that the progress you've made becomes a permanent part of your daily routine. This transition is about maintaining the momentum you've built while allowing for the flexibility needed to enjoy a balanced, fulfilling life.

Embracing Flexibility and Mindfulness

One of the most important aspects of transitioning to a long-term lifestyle is learning to embrace flexibility. The meal plans provided structure and discipline, but a sustainable approach to eating must accommodate the varied and unpredictable nature of everyday life. This doesn't mean abandoning the principles you've followed; rather, it's about adapting them to fit a more fluid routine.

Begin by incorporating more variety into your meals, allowing yourself to experiment with new foods and flavors while maintaining the nutritional balance that served you well during the plan. The goal is to enjoy a diverse diet that nourishes your body without feeling restrictive. This flexibility also extends to social situations and special occasions—learning to enjoy these moments mindfully, without guilt, is key to long-term success.

Continuing Core Habits

While flexibility is essential, the core habits you've developed should remain the cornerstone of your lifestyle. Continue meal prepping, as it helps you stay organized and reduces the temptation to make unhealthy choices. Mindful eating should also remain a priority—pay attention to your hunger and fullness cues, and take the time to savor your meals.

Regular physical activity is another habit that should carry over. Whether it's maintaining your current exercise routine or trying new activities, staying active is crucial for both physical and mental well-being. Consistency in these habits will help you maintain the progress you've made and continue to build on it.

Setting Long-Term Goals

As you transition, it's helpful to set long-term goals that align with your new lifestyle. These goals should be realistic, focusing on maintaining your current weight, improving your fitness, or continuing to enhance your overall health. Setting goals keeps you motivated and gives you a clear path forward, helping to prevent the complacency that can sometimes follow a structured plan.

These goals can also evolve over time. As you settle into your new routine, you may find that your priorities shift—perhaps you'll want to focus on building strength, exploring new types of physical activity, or improving specific aspects of your nutrition. Allow yourself the flexibility to adapt your goals as you grow.

Preparing for life after the meal plan is about creating a lifestyle that's both sustainable and enjoyable. By embracing flexibility, continuing the core habits you've established, and setting long-term goals, you can transition smoothly from a structured plan to a balanced approach that supports your health and well-being for the long term. This is not the end of your journey but the beginning of a new chapter, one where the habits and lessons you've learned become the foundation for a vibrant, healthy life.

6.5.3 CELEBRATING YOUR SUCCESS

As you approach the end of your five-week meal plan, it's time to step back and truly acknowledge the journey you've undertaken. Celebrating your success is an essential part of this process, not just as a way to recognize your achievements but also to reinforce the positive changes you've made. This celebration marks the culmination of your hard work, but it also sets the stage for the goals you'll continue to pursue in the future.

Recognizing Your Achievements

First and foremost, take a moment to reflect on how far you've come. Think about the initial challenges you faced in the first week, the habits you've developed, and the progress you've made—whether that's measured in pounds lost, inches trimmed, or simply the way you feel in your own skin. Every step forward is a victory worth celebrating, and it's important to give yourself credit for the dedication and perseverance you've shown.

This recognition isn't just about the physical changes; it's also about the mental and emotional growth you've experienced. Perhaps you've developed a healthier relationship with food, found new ways to manage stress, or gained confidence in your ability to set and achieve goals. These are all significant accomplishments that contribute to your overall well-being and set a strong foundation for the future.

Rewarding Yourself

As part of celebrating your success, consider rewarding yourself in a way that aligns with your new lifestyle. This doesn't necessarily mean indulging in food-related treats, but rather finding ways to acknowledge your efforts that reinforce your healthy habits. Maybe it's investing in new workout gear, treating yourself to a relaxing day at the spa, or even planning an activity you've always wanted to try.

The key is to choose a reward that feels meaningful and that encourages you to continue your journey. Rewards are not just about immediate gratification; they serve as positive reinforcement, reminding you that your hard work is valued and worth continuing.

Setting Future Goals

While celebrating your current success, it's also important to look ahead and set new goals. The end of the five-week plan is not the end of your journey—it's a milestone along a much longer path. Consider what you'd like to achieve next, whether it's maintaining your current progress, setting new fitness goals, or continuing to refine your nutrition.

Your future goals should be realistic and attainable, yet challenging enough to keep you motivated. As you set these goals, remember the strategies and habits that have served you well so far, and think about how you can build on them. These goals will help keep your momentum going, ensuring that the progress you've made is not just temporary, but a permanent part of your lifestyle.

Celebrating your success is about more than just acknowledging your achievements; it's about reinforcing the positive changes you've made and setting yourself up for continued growth. By recognizing your progress, rewarding yourself in meaningful ways, and setting future goals, you create a powerful sense of accomplishment that fuels your journey forward. This celebration is not just an end, but a beginning—a stepping stone toward a vibrant, healthy life that you've worked hard to build and are now ready to sustain.

7.1 QUICK AND NUTRITIOUS BREAKFAST OPTIONS

GREEK YOGURT PARFAIT WITH BERRIES & ALMONDS

PREPARATION TIME: 5 min.

COOKING TIME: None

SERVINGS: 2 servings

TARGETED INGREDIENTS:

- 1 cup non-fat Greek yogurt (high in protein, low in fat)
- 1/2 cup mixed berries (antioxidants, low in calories)
- 1 Tbsp sliced almonds (healthy fats, fiber)
- 1 tsp honey (optional, natural sweetness)

INSTRUCTIONS FOCUSED ON DR. NOWZARADAN'S PLAN:

1. **Start with Protein:** Spoon 1 cup of non-fat Greek yogurt into a bowl or jar. Greek yogurt provides a solid base of protein without adding unnecessary fats.

2. **Add Nutrient-Dense Berries:** Layer 1/2 cup of mixed berries over the yogurt. Berries are low in calories and high in vitamins, providing a nutrient boost.

3. **Include Healthy Fats:** Sprinkle 1 Tbsp of sliced almonds on top for healthy fats and added crunch, which helps keep you full longer.

4. **Optional Sweetness:** Drizzle 1 tsp of honey if desired, though it's optional to keep the sugar content low.

TIPS FOR QUICK AND SUSTAINABLE PREPARATION:

- **Batch Prep:** Prepare multiple parfaits at once in jars, ready to grab and go during the week.

ADAPTATIONS FOR LONG-TERM SUCCESS:

- **Balanced Nutrition:** This recipe provides a balance of protein, healthy fats, and natural sugars, making it a sustainable breakfast option.

- **Sustainability:** Easy to prepare in advance and customize with different fruits and nuts to keep it exciting.

NUTRITIONAL VALUES:

Calories: 180 kcal | Protein: 0.7 oz | Carbohydrates: 0.6 oz | Fiber: 0.1 oz | Fat: 0.2 oz (primarily from almonds)

AVOCADO & EGG TOAST

PREPARATION TIME: 5 min.

COOKING TIME: 5 min.

SERVINGS: 2 servings

TARGETED INGREDIENTS:

- 1 slice whole-grain bread (fiber, complex carbohydrates)
- 1/2 avocado (healthy fats, fiber)
- 1 large egg (lean protein)
- Salt and pepper to taste (use sparingly to control sodium intake)
- A squeeze of lemon juice (optional, for flavor)

INSTRUCTIONS FOCUSED ON DR. NOWZARADAN'S PLAN:

1. **Toast the Bread:** Toast 1 slice of whole-grain bread to your preferred level of crispiness. Whole grains provide complex carbohydrates and fiber to keep you satisfied.

2. **Prepare the Avocado:** Mash 1/2 avocado with a fork, adding a squeeze of lemon juice if desired. Spread it evenly over the toast.

3. **Cook the Egg:** In a non-stick pan, cook 1 large egg to your liking (poached, scrambled, or fried with minimal oil). Eggs provide high-quality protein without excessive fat.

4. **Assemble & Season:** Place the cooked egg on top of the avocado toast. Season with salt and pepper to taste, but use sparingly to control sodium.

TIPS FOR QUICK AND SUSTAINABLE PREPARATION:

- **Time Saver:** Cook the egg while the bread is toasting to save time.

ADAPTATIONS FOR LONG-TERM SUCCESS:

- **Balanced Nutrition:** This recipe combines healthy fats, fiber, and lean protein, aligning with Dr. Nowzaradan's plan.
- **Sustainability:** Simple and quick to prepare, making it easy to incorporate into a busy morning routine.

NUTRITIONAL VALUES:

Calories: 250 kcal | Protein: 0.7 oz | Carbohydrates: 1 oz | Fiber: 0.3 oz | Fat: 0.6 oz (primarily from avocado)

BERRY & OAT SMOOTHIE

PREPARATION TIME: 5 min.
COOKING TIME: None
SERVINGS: 2 servings
TARGETED INGREDIENTS:

- 1/2 cup rolled oats (fiber, complex carbohydrates)
- 1/2 cup unsweetened almond milk (low-calorie, dairy-free)
- 1/2 cup mixed berries (antioxidants, low in calories)
- 1 scoop protein powder (optional, for additional protein)
- 1 tsp honey or stevia (optional, natural sweetener)

INSTRUCTIONS FOCUSED ON DR. NOWZARADAN'S PLAN:

1. **Start with Fiber:** Add 1/2 cup of rolled oats to a blender. Oats provide fiber to keep you full and support digestion.

2. **Add Liquid:** Pour in 1/2 cup of unsweetened almond milk. Almond milk is a low-calorie option that keeps the smoothie light.

3. **Incorporate Nutrient-Dense Ingredients:** Add 1/2 cup of mixed berries for flavor and antioxidants. Optionally, add a scoop of protein powder for an extra protein boost.

4. **Blend:** Blend until smooth, adding a tsp of honey or stevia if needed for sweetness.

TIPS FOR QUICK AND SUSTAINABLE PREPARATION:

- **Make-Ahead:** Prepare the dry ingredients in smoothie packs, ready to blend with liquid in the morning.

ADAPTATIONS FOR LONG-TERM SUCCESS:

- **Balanced Nutrition:** This smoothie offers a balanced combination of fiber, antioxidants, and protein, supporting weight loss and energy.

- **Sustainability:** Easily customizable with different fruits or protein powders to keep breakfast interesting.

NUTRITIONAL VALUES:

Calories: 200 kcal | Protein: 0.7 oz | Carbohydrates: 1 oz | Fiber: 0.3 oz | Fat: 0.2 oz

VEGGIE & EGG MUFFINS

PREPARATION TIME: 10 min.
COOKING TIME: 20 min.
SERVINGS: 2 servings
TARGETED INGREDIENTS:

- 6 large eggs (lean protein)
- 1 cup chopped spinach (low carb, rich in iron and vitamins)
- 1/2 cup diced bell peppers (low-calorie, high in vitamins)
- 1/4 cup low-fat cheese (optional, for flavor without excess fat)
- Salt and pepper to taste (use sparingly to control sodium intake)
- Cooking spray (reduced calories compared to oil)

INSTRUCTIONS FOCUSED ON DR. NOWZARADAN'S PLAN:

1. **Preheat & Prep:** Preheat the oven to 350°F (175°C). Spray a muffin tin with cooking spray to reduce sticking without adding unnecessary calories.
2. **Mix the Ingredients:** In a large bowl, whisk 6 large eggs. Add 1 cup chopped spinach, 1/2 cup diced bell peppers, and 1/4 cup low-fat cheese if using. Season with salt and pepper.
3. **Pour & Bake:** Pour the egg mixture evenly into the muffin tin, filling each cup about 3/4 full. Bake for 20 minutes, or until the eggs are set and slightly golden on top.

TIPS FOR QUICK AND SUSTAINABLE PREPARATION:

- **Batch Cooking:** These muffins can be made in large batches and stored in the refrigerator for quick breakfasts throughout the week.

ADAPTATIONS FOR LONG-TERM SUCCESS:

- **Balanced Nutrition:** These egg muffins provide a convenient, portable source of protein and vegetables.
- **Sustainability:** They can be customized with various vegetables and proteins to suit your tastes and keep breakfast varied.

NUTRITIONAL VALUES:

Calories: 120 kcal (per muffin) | Protein: 0.7 oz | Carbohydrates: 0.2 oz | Fiber: 0.1 oz | Fat: 0.3 oz

COTTAGE CHEESE & PINEAPPLE BOWL

PREPARATION TIME: 5 min.
COOKING TIME: None
SERVINGS: 2 servings
TARGETED INGREDIENTS:

- 1 cup low-fat cottage cheese (high in protein, low in fat)
- 1/2 cup fresh pineapple chunks (natural sweetness, digestive enzymes)
- 1 Tbsp chia seeds (fiber, omega-3 fatty acids)
- A sprinkle of cinnamon (optional, for flavor)

INSTRUCTIONS FOCUSED ON DR. NOWZARADAN'S PLAN:

1. **Start with Protein:** Spoon 1 cup of low-fat cottage cheese into a bowl. Cottage cheese is rich in protein and helps keep you full.
2. **Add Natural Sweetness:** Top with 1/2 cup of fresh pineapple chunks. Pineapple adds natural sweetness without refined sugar and provides digestive benefits.
3. **Boost with Fiber:** Sprinkle 1 Tbsp of chia seeds over the top for added fiber and omega-3 fatty acids.

4. **Optional Flavor:** Add a sprinkle of cinnamon if desired for extra flavor and potential blood sugar regulation.

TIPS FOR QUICK AND SUSTAINABLE PREPARATION:

- **Meal Prep:** Prepare the pineapple and chia seeds in advance so you can assemble the bowl in under a minute.

ADAPTATIONS FOR LONG-TERM SUCCESS:

- **Balanced Nutrition:** This recipe balances protein, natural sugars, and healthy fats, making it a satisfying breakfast option.
- **Sustainability:** Easy to prepare and adaptable with different fruits or seeds for variety.

NUTRITIONAL VALUES:

Calories: 220 kcal | Protein: 0.7 oz | Carbohydrates: 1 oz | Fiber: 0.2 oz | Fat: 0.3 oz

ALMOND BUTTER & BANANA WRAP

PREPARATION TIME: 5 min.
COOKING TIME: None
SERVINGS: 2 servings

TARGETED INGREDIENTS:

- 1 whole-grain tortilla (fiber, complex carbohydrates)
- 1 Tbsp almond butter (healthy fats, protein)
- 1 small banana (natural sugars, potassium)
- A sprinkle of flaxseeds (optional, for added fiber)

INSTRUCTIONS FOCUSED ON DR. NOWZARADAN'S PLAN:

1. **Start with a Healthy Base:** Place a whole-grain tortilla on a flat surface. Whole grains provide complex carbohydrates and fiber for sustained energy.
2. **Add Healthy Fats:** Spread 1 Tbsp of almond butter evenly over the tortilla. Almond butter adds healthy fats and protein to keep you full.

3. **Incorporate Natural Sweetness:** Peel and place a small banana in the center of the tortilla. The banana provides natural sweetness and is rich in potassium.
4. **Optional Fiber Boost:** Sprinkle a few flaxseeds over the banana if desired.
5. **Wrap & Serve:** Roll the tortilla tightly around the banana and almond butter. Cut in half if preferred.

TIPS FOR QUICK AND SUSTAINABLE PREPARATION:

- **On-the-Go:** This wrap is perfect for a quick, portable breakfast when you're short on time.

ADAPTATIONS FOR LONG-TERM SUCCESS:

- **Balanced Nutrition:** This wrap provides a balance of fiber, protein, and healthy fats, making it a filling breakfast.
- **Sustainability:** Simple to prepare and adaptable with different nut butters or fruits.

NUTRITIONAL VALUES:

Calories: 240 kcal | Protein: 0.6 oz | Carbohydrates: 1.5 oz | Fiber: 0.4 oz | Fat: 0.4 oz

EGG & VEGGIE BREAKFAST BURRITO

PREPARATION TIME: 10 min.
COOKING TIME: 10 min.
SERVINGS: 2 servings

TARGETED INGREDIENTS:

- 2 large eggs (lean protein)
- 1/4 cup black beans (fiber, plant-based protein)
- 1/4 cup diced tomatoes (low-calorie, high in vitamins)
- 1/4 cup chopped bell peppers (rich in vitamins, low in calories)
- 1 whole-grain tortilla (fiber, complex carbohydrates)
- 1 Tbsp salsa (optional, for flavor without excess calories)

- Salt and pepper to taste (use sparingly to control sodium intake)

INSTRUCTIONS FOCUSED ON DR. NOWZARADAN'S PLAN:

1. **Cook the Eggs:** In a non-stick pan, scramble 2 large eggs. Eggs provide high-quality protein without excessive fat.
2. **Prepare the Veggies:** Add 1/4 cup diced tomatoes, 1/4 cup chopped bell peppers, and 1/4 cup black beans to the pan. Cook for 2-3 minutes, until the vegetables are tender.
3. **Assemble the Burrito:** Place the cooked egg and veggie mixture into a whole-grain tortilla. Whole grains provide fiber and complex carbohydrates for sustained energy.
4. **Optional Flavor Boost:** Add 1 Tbsp of salsa for extra flavor, keeping it low-calorie.
5. **Wrap & Serve:** Roll the tortilla tightly to form a burrito. Serve immediately.

TIPS FOR QUICK AND SUSTAINABLE PREPARATION:

- **Batch Cooking:** Prepare the egg and veggie mixture in advance, so you only need to assemble the burrito in the morning.

ADAPTATIONS FOR LONG-TERM SUCCESS:

- **Balanced Nutrition:** This burrito offers a balanced combination of protein, fiber, and vegetables.
- **Sustainability:** Easily customizable with different vegetables or protein sources to keep it varied.

NUTRITIONAL VALUES:

Calories: 280 kcal | Protein: 0.8 oz | Carbohydrates: 1.6 oz | Fiber: 0.5 oz | Fat: 0.4 oz

7.2 HIGH-PROTEIN BREAKFASTS

TURKEY & EGG WHITE BREAKFAST WRAP

PREPARATION TIME: 5 min.

COOKING TIME: 5 min.

SERVINGS: 2 servings

TARGETED INGREDIENTS:

- 4 egg whites (lean protein, low in fat)
- 2 oz sliced turkey breast (lean protein)
- 1 whole-grain tortilla (fiber, complex carbohydrates)
- 1/4 cup baby spinach (low carb, rich in iron and vitamins)
- 1 Tbsp salsa (optional, low-calorie flavor)
- Salt and pepper to taste (use sparingly to control sodium intake)

INSTRUCTIONS FOCUSED ON DR. NOWZARADAN'S PLAN:

1. **Cook the Egg Whites:** In a non-stick pan, cook 4 egg whites over medium heat until fully set. Egg whites are a great source of protein without added fat.
2. **Warm the Tortilla:** While the egg whites cook, warm a whole-grain tortilla in another pan or microwave.
3. **Assemble the Wrap:** Lay the cooked egg whites on the tortilla, followed by 2 oz of sliced turkey breast and 1/4 cup of baby spinach. Add 1 Tbsp of salsa if desired.
4. **Season & Serve:** Season with salt and pepper to taste, then wrap the tortilla tightly. Serve immediately.

TIPS FOR QUICK AND SUSTAINABLE PREPARATION:

- **Make-Ahead:** Prepare the filling the night before, so you only need to warm the tortilla and assemble in the morning.

ADAPTATIONS FOR LONG-TERM SUCCESS:

- **Balanced Nutrition:** This wrap combines lean protein and fiber for a satisfying breakfast that supports weight loss.
- **Sustainability:** Simple to prepare and easy to customize with different vegetables or lean proteins.

NUTRITIONAL VALUES:

Calories: 220 kcal | Protein: 1.1 oz | Carbohydrates: 0.8 oz | Fiber: 0.2 oz | Fat: 0.1 oz

COTTAGE CHEESE & BERRY PROTEIN BOWL

PREPARATION TIME: 5 min.
COOKING TIME: None
SERVINGS: 2 servings
TARGETED INGREDIENTS:

- 1 cup low-fat cottage cheese (high in protein, low in fat)
- 1/2 cup mixed berries (antioxidants, low in calories)
- 1 Tbsp chia seeds (fiber, omega-3 fatty acids)
- A sprinkle of cinnamon (optional, for flavor)

INSTRUCTIONS FOCUSED ON DR. NOWZARADAN'S PLAN:

1. **Start with Protein:** Spoon 1 cup of low-fat cottage cheese into a bowl. Cottage cheese is rich in protein, which keeps you full and satisfied.
2. **Add Nutrient-Dense Toppings:** Top with 1/2 cup of mixed berries for natural sweetness and antioxidants. Add 1 Tbsp of chia seeds for extra fiber and omega-3 fatty acids.
3. **Optional Flavor:** Sprinkle with cinnamon if desired, which may help regulate blood sugar levels.

TIPS FOR QUICK AND SUSTAINABLE PREPARATION:

- **Quick Prep:** Assemble the night before for a grab-and-go breakfast in the morning.

ADAPTATIONS FOR LONG-TERM SUCCESS:

- **Balanced Nutrition:** This bowl offers a balanced combination of protein, fiber, and healthy fats, making it a perfect high-protein breakfast.
- **Sustainability:** Easily customizable with different fruits and seeds to keep it fresh and exciting.

NUTRITIONAL VALUES:

Calories: 220 kcal | Protein: 1.1 oz | Carbohydrates: 0.7 oz | Fiber: 0.2 oz | Fat: 0.3 oz

SMOKED SALMON & AVOCADO TOAST

PREPARATION TIME: 5 min.
COOKING TIME: 5 min.
SERVINGS: 2 servings
TARGETED INGREDIENTS:

- 2 oz smoked salmon (high in protein, rich in omega-3 fatty acids)
- 1/2 avocado (healthy fats, fiber)
- 1 slice whole-grain bread (fiber, complex carbohydrates)
- 1/4 lemon (for flavor)
- Salt and pepper to taste (use sparingly to control sodium intake)

INSTRUCTIONS FOCUSED ON DR. NOWZARADAN'S PLAN:

1. **Toast the Bread:** Start by toasting a slice of whole-grain bread, which provides fiber and complex carbohydrates.
2. **Prepare the Avocado:** Mash 1/2 avocado and spread it evenly over the toast. Avocado offers healthy fats that help keep you full.
3. **Add Protein:** Layer 2 oz of smoked salmon over the avocado. Salmon is rich in protein and omega-3 fatty acids.
4. **Season & Serve:** Squeeze 1/4 lemon over the top, and season with salt and pepper to taste.

TIPS FOR QUICK AND SUSTAINABLE PREPARATION:

- **On-the-Go:** Prepare all ingredients in advance for a quick assembly in the morning.

ADAPTATIONS FOR LONG-TERM SUCCESS:

- **Balanced Nutrition:** This recipe combines protein, healthy fats, and fiber, supporting a balanced, high-protein breakfast.
- **Sustainability:** Easy to prepare and versatile, with the option to add different toppings like tomato slices or cucumber.

NUTRITIONAL VALUES:

Calories: 270 kcal | Protein: 1.2 oz | Carbohydrates: 0.8 oz | Fiber: 0.3 oz | Fat: 0.6 oz

GREEK YOGURT & ALMOND BUTTER PARFAIT

PREPARATION TIME: 5 min.

COOKING TIME: None

SERVINGS: 2 servings

TARGETED INGREDIENTS:

- 1 cup non-fat Greek yogurt (high in protein, low in fat)
- 1 Tbsp almond butter (healthy fats, protein)
- 1/2 cup mixed berries (antioxidants, low in calories)
- 1 Tbsp sliced almonds (optional, for added crunch and healthy fats)

INSTRUCTIONS FOCUSED ON DR. NOWZARADAN'S PLAN:

1. **Start with Protein:** Spoon 1 cup of non-fat Greek yogurt into a bowl. Greek yogurt is high in protein and low in fat, making it an ideal breakfast base.
2. **Add Healthy Fats:** Swirl 1 Tbsp of almond butter into the yogurt for healthy fats and additional protein.
3. **Top with Nutrient-Dense Ingredients:** Add 1/2 cup of mixed berries for natural sweetness and antioxidants. Optionally,

sprinkle 1 Tbsp of sliced almonds for added crunch.

TIPS FOR QUICK AND SUSTAINABLE PREPARATION:

- **Make-Ahead:** Prepare multiple parfaits in jars for a quick grab-and-go breakfast during the week.

ADAPTATIONS FOR LONG-TERM SUCCESS:

- **Balanced Nutrition:** This parfait offers a combination of protein, healthy fats, and natural sugars, making it both satisfying and nutritious.
- **Sustainability:** Easily customizable with different nut butters or fruits to keep breakfast interesting.

NUTRITIONAL VALUES:

Calories: 250 kcal | Protein: 1.0 oz | Carbohydrates: 0.7 oz | Fiber: 0.2 oz | Fat: 0.6 oz

QUINOA BREAKFAST BOWL WITH EGGS

PREPARATION TIME: 10 min.

COOKING TIME: 15 min.

SERVINGS: 2 servings

TARGETED INGREDIENTS:

- 1/2 cup cooked quinoa (complete protein, fiber)
- 2 large eggs (lean protein)
- 1/4 avocado (healthy fats, fiber)
- 1/4 cup cherry tomatoes (low-calorie, high in vitamins)
- Salt and pepper to taste (use sparingly to control sodium intake)
- 1 tsp olive oil (optional, for cooking)

INSTRUCTIONS FOCUSED ON DR. NOWZARADAN'S PLAN:

1. **Cook the Quinoa:** Prepare 1/2 cup of quinoa according to package instructions. Quinoa is a

complete protein and a great base for this high-protein bowl.

2. **Cook the Eggs:** In a non-stick pan, cook 2 large eggs to your preference (scrambled, fried, or poached). Eggs add lean protein to the meal.

3. **Assemble the Bowl:** In a bowl, layer the cooked quinoa, eggs, 1/4 sliced avocado, and 1/4 cup halved cherry tomatoes.

4. **Season & Serve:** Drizzle with 1 tsp of olive oil if desired, and season with salt and pepper to taste.

TIPS FOR QUICK AND SUSTAINABLE PREPARATION:

- **Batch Cooking:** Prepare a larger batch of quinoa ahead of time to save time in the morning.

ADAPTATIONS FOR LONG-TERM SUCCESS:

- **Balanced Nutrition:** This breakfast bowl offers a mix of complete protein, healthy fats, and fiber, making it a balanced and sustaining option.
- **Sustainability:** Easily customizable with different vegetables or proteins, allowing for variety.

NUTRITIONAL VALUES:

Calories: 300 kcal | Protein: 1.1 oz | Carbohydrates: 1.1 oz | Fiber: 0.4 oz | Fat: 0.7 oz

PROTEIN PANCAKES WITH BERRIES

PREPARATION TIME: 10 min.
COOKING TIME: 10 min.
SERVINGS: 2 servings
TARGETED INGREDIENTS:

- 1 scoop protein powder (high in protein)
- 1/4 cup rolled oats (fiber, complex carbohydrates)
- 1/4 cup egg whites (lean protein, low in fat)

- 1/4 cup unsweetened almond milk (low-calorie, dairy-free)
- 1/2 tsp baking powder (for fluffiness)
- 1/2 cup mixed berries (antioxidants, low in calories)
- Cooking spray (for cooking)

INSTRUCTIONS FOCUSED ON DR. NOWZARADAN'S PLAN:

1. **Mix the Ingredients:** In a blender, combine 1 scoop of protein powder, 1/4 cup rolled oats, 1/4 cup egg whites, 1/4 cup unsweetened almond milk, and 1/2 tsp baking powder. Blend until smooth.

2. **Cook the Pancakes:** Heat a non-stick pan over medium heat and spray lightly with cooking spray. Pour the batter into the pan to form pancakes, cooking for 2-3 minutes on each side until golden brown.

3. **Serve with Berries:** Top with 1/2 cup of mixed berries for natural sweetness and antioxidants.

TIPS FOR QUICK AND SUSTAINABLE PREPARATION:

- **Batch Cooking:** Make a large batch of pancakes and freeze for a quick breakfast option during the week.

ADAPTATIONS FOR LONG-TERM SUCCESS:

- **Balanced Nutrition:** These protein-packed pancakes provide a mix of protein and fiber, keeping you full and energized.
- **Sustainability:** Simple to prepare and customizable with different toppings to keep breakfast exciting.

NUTRITIONAL VALUES:

Calories: 260 kcal | Protein: 1.2 oz | Carbohydrates: 1.0 oz | Fiber: 0.3 oz | Fat: 0.3 oz

TOFU SCRAMBLE WITH VEGGIES

PREPARATION TIME: 10 min.
COOKING TIME: 10 min.
SERVINGS: 2 servings
TARGETED INGREDIENTS:

- 4 oz firm tofu (high in protein, low in fat)
- 1/4 cup diced bell peppers (low-calorie, high in vitamins)
- 1/4 cup chopped spinach (low carb, rich in iron and vitamins)
- 1/4 tsp turmeric (optional, for color and anti-inflammatory benefits)
- 1 tsp olive oil (optional, for cooking)
- Salt and pepper to taste (use sparingly to control sodium intake)

INSTRUCTIONS FOCUSED ON DR. NOWZARADAN'S PLAN:

1. **Prepare the Tofu:** Drain and crumble 4 oz of firm tofu into a bowl. Tofu is a great plant-based protein source.
2. **Cook the Vegetables:** In a non-stick pan, heat 1 tsp of olive oil over medium heat. Add 1/4 cup diced bell peppers and cook until softened, about 3 minutes. Add 1/4 cup chopped spinach and cook for an additional 2 minutes.
3. **Add the Tofu:** Add the crumbled tofu to the pan, along with 1/4 tsp turmeric if using. Cook for 5 minutes, stirring occasionally, until the tofu is heated through and the turmeric has evenly coated the mixture.
4. **Season & Serve:** Season with salt and pepper to taste, and serve immediately.

TIPS FOR QUICK AND SUSTAINABLE PREPARATION:

- **Batch Cooking:** Prepare a larger batch and store in the refrigerator for up to three days, reheating as needed.

ADAPTATIONS FOR LONG-TERM SUCCESS:

- **Balanced Nutrition:** This tofu scramble is rich in protein and fiber, providing a filling, plant-based breakfast option.
- **Sustainability:** Easily customizable with different vegetables and spices, keeping breakfast varied and interesting.

NUTRITIONAL VALUES:

Calories: 220 kcal | Protein: 1.0 oz | Carbohydrates: 0.5 oz | Fiber: 0.2 oz | Fat: 0.4 oz

7.3 LOW-CARB BREAKFAST IDEAS

AVOCADO & BACON EGG CUPS

PREPARATION TIME: 5 min.
COOKING TIME: 15 min.
SERVINGS: 2 servings
TARGETED INGREDIENTS:

- 2 medium avocados (healthy fats, fiber)
- 4 large eggs (lean protein)
- 2 slices turkey bacon (low-fat, high-protein alternative to regular bacon)
- Salt and pepper to taste (use sparingly to control sodium intake)
- A pinch of paprika (optional, for flavor)

INSTRUCTIONS FOCUSED ON DR. NOWZARADAN'S PLAN:

1. **Preheat Oven:** Preheat your oven to 375°F (190°C).
2. **Prepare the Avocados:** Slice each avocado in half and remove the pits. Scoop out a small portion of the avocado flesh to create space for the egg.
3. **Cook the Bacon:** Cook 2 slices of turkey bacon in a pan over medium heat until crisp. Once cooked, crumble into small pieces.
4. **Fill the Avocado:** Place the avocado halves in a baking dish, ensuring they are stable. Crack

an egg into each avocado half, filling the space where the pit was.

5. **Add Bacon & Season:** Sprinkle the crumbled bacon over the eggs. Season with salt, pepper, and a pinch of paprika if desired.

6. **Bake:** Bake in the preheated oven for 12-15 minutes, or until the eggs are cooked to your preference.

7. **Serve:** Remove from the oven and serve immediately.

TIPS FOR QUICK AND SUSTAINABLE PREPARATION:

- **Advance Prep:** Prepare the avocados and bacon ahead of time, so you only need to crack the eggs and bake in the morning.

ADAPTATIONS FOR LONG-TERM SUCCESS:

- **Balanced Nutrition:** This recipe offers a satisfying combination of protein and healthy fats, making it a great low-carb breakfast option.

- **Sustainability:** Simple and easy to customize with different spices or even add a small portion of lean protein like smoked salmon.

NUTRITIONAL VALUES:

Calories: 300 kcal | Protein: 0.9 oz | Carbohydrates: 0.3 oz | Fiber: 0.4 oz | Fat: 1.5 oz

CAULIFLOWER HASH BROWNS

PREPARATION TIME: 10 min.
COOKING TIME: 20 min.
SERVINGS: 2 servings
TARGETED INGREDIENTS:

- 1 small head of cauliflower (low-carb, fiber-rich)
- 1 large egg (lean protein)
- 1/4 cup grated low-fat cheddar cheese (adds flavor without excessive calories)
- 1 Tbsp almond flour (low-carb binding agent)

- Salt and pepper to taste (use sparingly to control sodium intake)
- 1 tsp olive oil (optional, for cooking)

INSTRUCTIONS FOCUSED ON DR. NOWZARADAN'S PLAN:

1. **Preheat Oven:** Preheat your oven to 400°F (200°C) and line a baking sheet with parchment paper.

2. **Prepare the Cauliflower:** Grate the cauliflower into rice-sized pieces, then microwave for 3-4 minutes until soft. Let it cool slightly, then squeeze out excess moisture using a clean towel.

3. **Mix Ingredients:** In a bowl, combine the cauliflower, 1 large egg, 1/4 cup grated low-fat cheddar cheese, 1 Tbsp almond flour, salt, and pepper. Mix until well combined.

4. **Form Patties:** Form the mixture into small patties and place them on the prepared baking sheet.

5. **Bake:** Bake in the preheated oven for 15-20 minutes, flipping halfway through, until golden brown and crispy.

6. **Serve:** Serve immediately, either on their own or as a side to your favorite low-carb breakfast.

TIPS FOR QUICK AND SUSTAINABLE PREPARATION:

- **Batch Cooking:** Make a large batch and freeze for quick reheating throughout the week.

ADAPTATIONS FOR LONG-TERM SUCCESS:

- **Balanced Nutrition:** These hash browns provide a low-carb alternative to traditional potato-based versions, keeping you full without spiking blood sugar.

- **Sustainability:** Easy to prepare and can be enjoyed as part of various meals, making them versatile and convenient.

NUTRITIONAL VALUES:

Calories: 150 kcal | Protein: 0.5 oz | Carbohydrates: 0.2 oz | Fiber: 0.3 oz | Fat: 0.7 oz

ZUCCHINI NOODLES WITH PESTO & POACHED EGG

PREPARATION TIME: 10 min.
COOKING TIME: 10 min.
SERVINGS: 2 servings
TARGETED INGREDIENTS:

- 1 medium zucchini (low-carb, fiber-rich)
- 2 large eggs (lean protein)
- 1 Tbsp homemade or store-bought pesto (healthy fats, low-carb)
- Salt and pepper to taste (use sparingly to control sodium intake)
- 1 tsp olive oil (optional, for cooking)

INSTRUCTIONS FOCUSED ON DR. NOWZARADAN'S PLAN:

1. **Prepare the Zucchini Noodles:** Use a spiralizer to create zucchini noodles. If you don't have a spiralizer, you can slice the zucchini into thin strips.
2. **Cook the Noodles:** Heat 1 tsp of olive oil in a pan over medium heat. Add the zucchini noodles and cook for 2-3 minutes, until just tender. Remove from heat and toss with 1 Tbsp of pesto.
3. **Poach the Eggs:** Bring a pot of water to a gentle simmer. Crack each egg into a small bowl, then gently slide into the water. Poach for 3-4 minutes, until the whites are set but the yolks are still runny.
4. **Assemble the Dish:** Divide the pesto zucchini noodles between two plates. Top each with a poached egg.
5. **Serve:** Season with salt and pepper to taste, and serve immediately.

TIPS FOR QUICK AND SUSTAINABLE PREPARATION:

- **Make-Ahead:** Prepare the zucchini noodles and pesto in advance for a quick assembly in the morning.

ADAPTATIONS FOR LONG-TERM SUCCESS:

- **Balanced Nutrition:** This recipe combines low-carb zucchini noodles with lean protein and healthy fats, perfect for a satisfying, low-carb breakfast.
- **Sustainability:** Versatile and easy to adjust with different toppings like grilled chicken or turkey sausage for added variety.

NUTRITIONAL VALUES:

Calories: 200 kcal | Protein: 0.7 oz | Carbohydrates: 0.2 oz | Fiber: 0.3 oz | Fat: 0.8 oz

SPINACH & CHEESE STUFFED PORTOBELLO MUSHROOMS

PREPARATION TIME: 10 min.
COOKING TIME: 15 min.
SERVINGS: 2 servings
TARGETED INGREDIENTS:

- 2 large Portobello mushrooms (low-carb, nutrient-dense)
- 1/2 cup fresh spinach (low carb, rich in iron and vitamins)
- 1/4 cup low-fat ricotta or cottage cheese (high in protein, low in fat)
- 2 Tbsp grated Parmesan cheese (adds flavor without excess calories)
- Salt and pepper to taste (use sparingly to control sodium intake)
- 1 tsp olive oil (optional, for cooking)

INSTRUCTIONS FOCUSED ON DR. NOWZARADAN'S PLAN:

1. **Preheat Oven:** Preheat your oven to 375°F (190°C).
2. **Prepare the Mushrooms:** Remove the stems and gills from the Portobello mushrooms, then brush with 1 tsp olive oil if desired.

3. **Prepare the Filling:** In a bowl, mix 1/2 cup fresh spinach with 1/4 cup low-fat ricotta or cottage cheese. Season with salt and pepper.

4. **Stuff the Mushrooms:** Fill each mushroom cap with the spinach and cheese mixture. Top with 1 Tbsp grated Parmesan cheese.

5. **Bake:** Place the mushrooms on a baking sheet and bake in the preheated oven for 12-15 minutes, until the mushrooms are tender and the cheese is golden and bubbly.

6. **Serve:** Serve immediately, either on their own or with a side of scrambled eggs for an extra protein boost.

TIPS FOR QUICK AND SUSTAINABLE PREPARATION:

- **Batch Cooking:** Prepare a larger batch and reheat in the microwave or oven for quick breakfasts throughout the week.

ADAPTATIONS FOR LONG-TERM SUCCESS:

- **Balanced Nutrition:** These stuffed mushrooms offer a flavorful, low-carb option that's high in protein and nutrients.
- **Sustainability:** Easily adaptable with different cheeses or vegetables, making them a versatile and satisfying breakfast.

NUTRITIONAL VALUES:

Calories: 180 kcal | Protein: 0.8 oz | Carbohydrates: 0.2 oz | Fiber: 0.4 oz | Fat: 0.7 oz

SAUSAGE & EGG BREAKFAST SKILLET

PREPARATION TIME: 5 min.
COOKING TIME: 15 min.
SERVINGS: 2 servings
TARGETED INGREDIENTS:

- 4 oz turkey sausage (lean protein, low in fat)
- 4 large eggs (lean protein)
- 1/2 cup diced bell peppers (low-carb, high in vitamins)
- 1/4 cup chopped onion (adds flavor, low in calories)
- 1/4 cup shredded low-fat cheese (optional, for flavor without excess calories)
- Salt and pepper to taste (use sparingly to control sodium intake)
- 1 tsp olive oil (optional, for cooking)

INSTRUCTIONS FOCUSED ON DR. NOWZARADAN'S PLAN:

1. **Cook the Sausage:** In a non-stick skillet, cook 4 oz of turkey sausage over medium heat until browned. Remove from the skillet and set aside.

2. **Cook the Vegetables:** In the same skillet, add 1 tsp olive oil if desired, then cook 1/2 cup diced bell peppers and 1/4 cup chopped onion until softened, about 5 minutes.

3. **Add the Eggs:** Crack 4 large eggs into the skillet and scramble with the vegetables until the eggs are cooked through.

4. **Combine & Serve:** Add the cooked sausage back to the skillet and mix with the eggs and vegetables. Sprinkle with 1/4 cup shredded low-fat cheese if using. Season with salt and pepper to taste, and serve immediately.

TIPS FOR QUICK AND SUSTAINABLE PREPARATION:

- **Batch Cooking:** Make a larger portion and store in the refrigerator for a quick, reheat able breakfast.

ADAPTATIONS FOR LONG-TERM SUCCESS:

- **Balanced Nutrition:** This breakfast skillet is a protein-packed, low-carb meal that keeps you full and energized throughout the morning.
- **Sustainability:** Easy to prepare and adaptable with different vegetables or lean meats.

NUTRITIONAL VALUES:

Calories: 280 kcal | Protein: 1.2 oz | Carbohydrates: 0.3 oz | Fiber: 0.2 oz | Fat: 1.0 oz

GREEK YOGURT & FLAXSEED BOWL

PREPARATION TIME: 5 min.

COOKING TIME: None

SERVINGS: 2 servings

TARGETED INGREDIENTS:

- 1 cup plain Greek yogurt (high in protein, low in carbohydrates)
- 1 Tbsp ground flaxseeds (fiber, omega-3 fatty acids)
- 1/4 cup fresh raspberries (low-carb, antioxidants)
- 1/4 tsp cinnamon (optional, for flavor)

INSTRUCTIONS FOCUSED ON DR. NOWZARADAN'S PLAN:

1. **Start with Protein:** Spoon 1 cup of plain Greek yogurt into a bowl. Greek yogurt is rich in protein and low in carbs, making it an ideal breakfast base.
2. **Add Healthy Fats & Fiber:** Stir in 1 Tbsp of ground flaxseeds, which add fiber and omega-3 fatty acids.
3. **Top with Berries:** Add 1/4 cup of fresh raspberries for a touch of natural sweetness and antioxidants.
4. **Optional Flavor:** Sprinkle with 1/4 tsp cinnamon for added flavor and potential blood sugar regulation.

TIPS FOR QUICK AND SUSTAINABLE PREPARATION:

- **Make-Ahead:** Assemble the night before for a quick grab-and-go breakfast in the morning.

ADAPTATIONS FOR LONG-TERM SUCCESS:

- **Balanced Nutrition:** This bowl offers a combination of protein, fiber, and healthy fats, making it both satisfying and nutritious.

- **Sustainability:** Easily customizable with different fruits or seeds to keep breakfast varied and exciting.

NUTRITIONAL VALUES:

Calories: 200 kcal | Protein: 1.0 oz | Carbohydrates: 0.4 oz | Fiber: 0.3 oz | Fat: 0.5 oz

ALMOND FLOUR PANCAKES

PREPARATION TIME: 10 min.

COOKING TIME: 10 min.

SERVINGS: 2 servings

TARGETED INGREDIENTS:

- 1/2 cup almond flour (low-carb, high in healthy fats and fiber)
- 2 large eggs (lean protein)
- 1/4 cup unsweetened almond milk (low-calorie, dairy-free)
- 1/2 tsp baking powder (for fluffiness)
- 1/4 tsp vanilla extract (optional, for flavor)
- Cooking spray (for cooking)
- Fresh berries or sugar-free syrup (optional, for topping)

INSTRUCTIONS FOCUSED ON DR. NOWZARADAN'S PLAN:

1. **Mix the Ingredients:** In a bowl, combine 1/2 cup almond flour, 2 large eggs, 1/4 cup unsweetened almond milk, 1/2 tsp baking powder, and 1/4 tsp vanilla extract if using. Mix until smooth.
2. **Cook the Pancakes:** Heat a non-stick pan over medium heat and spray lightly with cooking spray. Pour the batter into the pan to form pancakes, cooking for 2-3 minutes on each side until golden brown.
3. **Serve:** Serve with fresh berries or a drizzle of sugar-free syrup if desired.

TIPS FOR QUICK AND SUSTAINABLE PREPARATION:

- **Batch Cooking:** Make a large batch and freeze for a quick breakfast option during the week.

ADAPTATIONS FOR LONG-TERM SUCCESS:

- **Balanced Nutrition:** These almond flour pancakes are a low-carb alternative to traditional pancakes, providing healthy fats and protein.

- **Sustainability:** Easy to prepare and customizable with different toppings to keep breakfast exciting.

NUTRITIONAL VALUES:

Calories: 250 kcal | Protein: 1.1 oz | Carbohydrates: 0.4 oz | Fiber: 0.3 oz | Fat: 1.0 oz

8.1 POWER SALADS: NUTRITIOUS AND SATISFYING

GRILLED CHICKEN & AVOCADO SALAD

PREPARATION TIME: 10 min.

COOKING TIME: 10 min.

SERVINGS: 2 servings

TARGETED INGREDIENTS:

- 4 oz grilled chicken breast (lean protein, low in fat)
- 1/2 avocado (healthy fats, fiber)
- 2 cups mixed greens (low-calorie, rich in vitamins and minerals)
- 1/4 cup cherry tomatoes (antioxidants, low in calories)
- 1 Tbsp olive oil (healthy fats)
- 1 Tbsp balsamic vinegar (low-calorie dressing option)
- Salt and pepper to taste (use sparingly to control sodium intake)

INSTRUCTIONS FOCUSED ON DR. NOWZARADAN'S PLAN:

1. **Grill the Chicken:** Season 4 oz of chicken breast with salt and pepper, then grill over medium heat for 4-5 minutes on each side until fully cooked. Let it rest for a few minutes before slicing.

2. **Prepare the Salad Base:** In a large bowl, combine 2 cups of mixed greens and 1/4 cup cherry tomatoes.

3. **Add Healthy Fats:** Slice 1/2 avocado and add it to the salad for healthy fats that keep you full longer.

4. **Top with Chicken:** Place the sliced grilled chicken on top of the salad.

5. **Dress the Salad:** Drizzle 1 Tbsp olive oil and 1 Tbsp balsamic vinegar over the salad. Toss gently to combine.

6. **Serve:** Serve immediately, either on its own or with a side of whole-grain crackers for added fiber.

TIPS FOR QUICK AND SUSTAINABLE PREPARATION:

- **Make-Ahead:** Grill extra chicken breast and store in the refrigerator for quick salad assembly throughout the week.

ADAPTATIONS FOR LONG-TERM SUCCESS:

- **Balanced Nutrition:** This salad offers a balance of lean protein, healthy fats, and fiber, making it a satisfying and nutritious lunch option.

- **Sustainability:** Simple to prepare and versatile, allowing you to change up the vegetables or proteins to keep it interesting.

NUTRITIONAL VALUES:

Calories: 350 kcal | Protein: 1.4 oz | Carbohydrates: 0.6 oz | Fiber: 0.3 oz | Fat: 1.2 oz

MEDITERRANEAN QUINOA SALAD

PREPARATION TIME: 15 min.

COOKING TIME: 15 min.

SERVINGS: 2 servings

TARGETED INGREDIENTS:

- 1/2 cup cooked quinoa (complete protein, fiber)
- 1/4 cup diced cucumber (hydrating, low in calories)
- 1/4 cup diced tomatoes (antioxidants, low in calories)
- 1/4 cup crumbled feta cheese (flavor without excess fat)
- 2 Tbsp Kalamata olives (healthy fats, rich in flavor)
- 1 Tbsp olive oil (healthy fats)
- 1 Tbsp lemon juice (low-calorie flavor boost)
- Salt and pepper to taste (use sparingly to control sodium intake)

INSTRUCTIONS FOCUSED ON DR. NOWZARADAN'S PLAN:

1. **Cook the Quinoa:** Prepare 1/2 cup of quinoa according to package instructions. Allow it to cool before assembling the salad.
2. **Prepare the Vegetables:** Dice 1/4 cup each of cucumber and tomatoes. Combine with the cooled quinoa in a large bowl.
3. **Add Flavorful Toppings:** Add 1/4 cup crumbled feta cheese and 2 Tbsp Kalamata olives to the quinoa mixture.
4. **Dress the Salad:** Drizzle 1 Tbsp olive oil and 1 Tbsp lemon juice over the salad. Toss gently to combine.
5. **Season & Serve:** Season with salt and pepper to taste. Serve immediately or chill in the refrigerator for a refreshing midday meal.

TIPS FOR QUICK AND SUSTAINABLE PREPARATION:

- **Batch Cooking:** Prepare a larger batch of quinoa to use in salads throughout the week.

ADAPTATIONS FOR LONG-TERM SUCCESS:

- **Balanced Nutrition:** This salad provides a complete protein source from quinoa, combined with healthy fats and fresh vegetables.
- **Sustainability:** Easy to prepare and store, making it a convenient option for busy days.

NUTRITIONAL VALUES:

Calories: 300 kcal | Protein: 1.0 oz | Carbohydrates: 1.2 oz | Fiber: 0.5 oz | Fat: 0.9 oz

SHRIMP & MANGO SPINACH SALAD

PREPARATION TIME: 10 min.

COOKING TIME: 5 min.

SERVINGS: 2 servings

TARGETED INGREDIENTS:

- 4 oz cooked shrimp (lean protein, low in fat)
- 1/2 cup diced mango (natural sweetness, vitamins)
- 2 cups baby spinach (low-calorie, rich in iron and vitamins)
- 1/4 avocado (healthy fats, fiber)
- 1 Tbsp lime juice (low-calorie flavor boost)
- 1 Tbsp olive oil (healthy fats)
- Salt and pepper to taste (use sparingly to control sodium intake)

INSTRUCTIONS FOCUSED ON DR. NOWZARADAN'S PLAN:

1. **Cook the Shrimp:** If not pre-cooked, sauté 4 oz of shrimp in a non-stick pan over medium heat for 2-3 minutes on each side until fully cooked. Set aside to cool slightly.
2. **Prepare the Salad Base:** In a large bowl, combine 2 cups of baby spinach and 1/2 cup diced mango.
3. **Add Healthy Fats:** Slice 1/4 avocado and add it to the salad for healthy fats that keep you satisfied.
4. **Top with Shrimp:** Add the cooked shrimp to the salad.
5. **Dress the Salad:** Drizzle 1 Tbsp olive oil and 1 Tbsp lime juice over the salad. Toss gently to combine.

6. **Serve:** Season with salt and pepper to taste and serve immediately.

TIPS FOR QUICK AND SUSTAINABLE PREPARATION:

- **Make-Ahead:** Prepare the shrimp and store in the refrigerator for quick salad assembly throughout the week.

ADAPTATIONS FOR LONG-TERM SUCCESS:

- **Balanced Nutrition:** This salad combines lean protein, healthy fats, and natural sweetness from the mango, making it both satisfying and nutritious.
- **Sustainability:** Simple to prepare and versatile, allowing you to change up the fruits or proteins to keep it interesting.

NUTRITIONAL VALUES:

Calories: 320 kcal | Protein: 1.2 oz | Carbohydrates: 0.8 oz | Fiber: 0.4 oz | Fat: 1.0 oz

TURKEY & KALE POWER SALAD

PREPARATION TIME: 10 min.
COOKING TIME: 5 min.
SERVINGS: 2 servings
TARGETED INGREDIENTS:

- 4 oz sliced turkey breast (lean protein, low in fat)
- 2 cups chopped kale (high in fiber, rich in vitamins)
- 1/4 cup shredded carrots (low-calorie, adds crunch)
- 1/4 cup cherry tomatoes (antioxidants, low in calories)
- 1 Tbsp pumpkin seeds (healthy fats, adds texture)
- 1 Tbsp olive oil (healthy fats)
- 1 Tbsp apple cider vinegar (low-calorie flavor boost)
- Salt and pepper to taste (use sparingly to control sodium intake)

INSTRUCTIONS FOCUSED ON DR. NOWZARADAN'S PLAN:

1. **Prepare the Kale:** In a large bowl, massage 2 cups of chopped kale with 1 Tbsp olive oil until tender.
2. **Add Vegetables:** Toss in 1/4 cup shredded carrots and 1/4 cup cherry tomatoes for added texture and nutrients.
3. **Top with Turkey:** Add 4 oz of sliced turkey breast to the salad for a lean protein boost.
4. **Include Healthy Fats:** Sprinkle 1 Tbsp of pumpkin seeds over the salad for healthy fats and added crunch.
5. **Dress the Salad:** Drizzle 1 Tbsp apple cider vinegar over the salad and toss gently to combine.
6. **Serve:** Season with salt and pepper to taste and serve immediately.

TIPS FOR QUICK AND SUSTAINABLE PREPARATION:

- **Advance Prep:** Massage the kale and store it in the refrigerator, so it's ready to assemble with the other ingredients when needed.

ADAPTATIONS FOR LONG-TERM SUCCESS:

- **Balanced Nutrition:** This salad offers a mix of lean protein, fiber, and healthy fats, making it a powerful and balanced midday meal.
- **Sustainability:** Easily customizable with different vegetables or seeds, ensuring variety and sustained interest.

NUTRITIONAL VALUES:

Calories: 280 kcal | Protein: 1.2 oz | Carbohydrates: 0.7 oz | Fiber: 0.5 oz | Fat: 0.9 oz

TOFU & BROCCOLI SALAD WITH SESAME DRESSING

PREPARATION TIME: 10 min.

COOKING TIME: 10 min.

SERVINGS: 2 servings

TARGETED INGREDIENTS:

- 4 oz firm tofu (high in protein, low in fat)
- 1 cup steamed broccoli (fiber, vitamins)
- 1/4 cup shredded carrots (low-calorie, adds color and nutrients)
- 1 Tbsp sesame seeds (healthy fats, adds flavor and texture)
- 1 Tbsp soy sauce (low-sodium version recommended)
- 1 Tbsp rice vinegar (low-calorie flavor boost)
- 1 tsp sesame oil (optional, for added flavor)
- Salt and pepper to taste (use sparingly to control sodium intake)

INSTRUCTIONS FOCUSED ON DR. NOWZARADAN'S PLAN:

1. **Prepare the Tofu:** Drain and press 4 oz of firm tofu to remove excess moisture, then cut into cubes.
2. **Cook the Tofu:** In a non-stick pan, sauté the tofu cubes over medium heat until golden brown on all sides, about 5-7 minutes.
3. **Steam the Broccoli:** Steam 1 cup of broccoli until tender but still vibrant green.
4. **Assemble the Salad:** In a large bowl, combine the tofu, steamed broccoli, and 1/4 cup shredded carrots.
5. **Add Sesame Dressing:** In a small bowl, mix 1 Tbsp soy sauce, 1 Tbsp rice vinegar, and 1 tsp sesame oil. Drizzle over the salad and toss gently to combine.
6. **Serve:** Sprinkle 1 Tbsp sesame seeds over the top, season with salt and pepper, and serve immediately.

TIPS FOR QUICK AND SUSTAINABLE PREPARATION:

- **Batch Cooking:** Prepare the tofu and vegetables ahead of time for quick salad assembly throughout the week.

ADAPTATIONS FOR LONG-TERM SUCCESS:

- **Balanced Nutrition:** This salad combines plant-based protein with fiber-rich vegetables, making it a nutritious and satisfying lunch option.
- **Sustainability:** Simple and versatile, allowing you to adjust the vegetables or dressing to keep it exciting.

NUTRITIONAL VALUES:

Calories: 270 kcal | Protein: 1.0 oz | Carbohydrates: 0.7 oz | Fiber: 0.4 oz | Fat: 1.1 oz

SALMON & ASPARAGUS SALAD

PREPARATION TIME: 10 min.

COOKING TIME: 15 min.

SERVINGS: 2 servings

TARGETED INGREDIENTS:

- 4 oz grilled salmon (high in protein, rich in omega-3 fatty acids)
- 1 cup steamed asparagus (low-carb, high in fiber and vitamins)
- 2 cups mixed greens (low-calorie, nutrient-dense)
- 1/4 cup cherry tomatoes (antioxidants, low in calories)
- 1 Tbsp olive oil (healthy fats)
- 1 Tbsp lemon juice (low-calorie flavor boost)
- Salt and pepper to taste (use sparingly to control sodium intake)

INSTRUCTIONS FOCUSED ON DR. NOWZARADAN'S PLAN:

1. **Grill the Salmon:** Season 4 oz of salmon with salt and pepper, then grill over medium heat for 4-5 minutes on each side until fully cooked.

Let it cool slightly before flaking into large pieces.

2. **Prepare the Salad Base:** In a large bowl, combine 2 cups of mixed greens, 1 cup steamed asparagus, and 1/4 cup cherry tomatoes.

3. **Add the Salmon:** Place the flaked salmon on top of the salad.

4. **Dress the Salad:** Drizzle 1 Tbsp olive oil and 1 Tbsp lemon juice over the salad. Toss gently to combine.

5. **Serve:** Season with salt and pepper to taste and serve immediately.

TIPS FOR QUICK AND SUSTAINABLE PREPARATION:

- **Advance Prep:** Grill extra salmon and store in the refrigerator for quick salad assembly throughout the week.

ADAPTATIONS FOR LONG-TERM SUCCESS:

- **Balanced Nutrition:** This salad provides a combination of lean protein, healthy fats, and fiber-rich vegetables, making it a balanced and satisfying meal.

- **Sustainability:** Simple to prepare and versatile, allowing you to switch up the vegetables or proteins for variety.

NUTRITIONAL VALUES:

Calories: 320 kcal | Protein: 1.4 oz | Carbohydrates: 0.6 oz | Fiber: 0.4 oz | Fat: 1.2 oz

LENTIL & BEETROOT SALAD WITH GOAT CHEESE

PREPARATION TIME: 15 min.
COOKING TIME: 20 min.
SERVINGS: 2 servings
TARGETED INGREDIENTS:

- 1/2 cup cooked lentils (high in protein, fiber-rich)
- 1/2 cup roasted beetroot (antioxidants, fiber)
- 2 cups arugula (low-calorie, nutrient-dense)

- 1 oz crumbled goat cheese (adds flavor without excessive calories)
- 1 Tbsp walnuts (healthy fats, adds crunch)
- 1 Tbsp balsamic vinegar (low-calorie dressing option)
- Salt and pepper to taste (use sparingly to control sodium intake)

INSTRUCTIONS FOCUSED ON DR. NOWZARADAN'S PLAN:

1. **Cook the Lentils:** Prepare 1/2 cup of lentils according to package instructions. Allow them to cool before assembling the salad.

2. **Prepare the Beetroot:** Roast 1/2 cup of beetroot until tender, then slice into bite-sized pieces.

3. **Assemble the Salad:** In a large bowl, combine 2 cups of arugula, cooked lentils, and roasted beetroot.

4. **Add Goat Cheese & Walnuts:** Sprinkle 1 oz of crumbled goat cheese and 1 Tbsp of walnuts over the salad.

5. **Dress the Salad:** Drizzle 1 Tbsp balsamic vinegar over the salad and toss gently to combine.

6. **Serve:** Season with salt and pepper to taste and serve immediately.

TIPS FOR QUICK AND SUSTAINABLE PREPARATION:

- **Batch Cooking:** Prepare the lentils and roast the beetroot in advance for quick salad assembly throughout the week.

ADAPTATIONS FOR LONG-TERM SUCCESS:

- **Balanced Nutrition:** This salad offers a combination of plant-based protein, fiber, and healthy fats, making it a nutritious and filling lunch option.

- **Sustainability:** Versatile and easy to adjust with different toppings or dressings to keep it fresh.

NUTRITIONAL VALUES:

Calories: 330 kcal | Protein: 1.0 oz | Carbohydrates: 1.2 oz | Fiber: 0.6 oz | Fat: 1.0 oz

---

8.2 LEAN AND LIGHT PROTEIN LUNCHES

LEMON HERB GRILLED CHICKEN WITH QUINOA

PREPARATION TIME: 10 min.

COOKING TIME: 15 min.

SERVINGS: 2 servings

TARGETED INGREDIENTS:

- 4 oz chicken breast (lean protein, low in fat)
- 1/2 cup cooked quinoa (complete protein, fiber-rich)
- 1 Tbsp olive oil (healthy fats)
- 1 Tbsp lemon juice (low-calorie flavor boost)
- 1 tsp fresh chopped herbs (parsley, thyme, or rosemary)
- 1 cup steamed broccoli (fiber, low-carb)
- Salt and pepper to taste (use sparingly to control sodium intake)

INSTRUCTIONS FOCUSED ON DR. NOWZARADAN'S PLAN:

1. **Prepare the Marinade:** In a bowl, mix 1 Tbsp olive oil, 1 Tbsp lemon juice, and 1 tsp chopped fresh herbs. Season with salt and pepper.
2. **Marinate the Chicken:** Coat 4 oz of chicken breast with the marinade and let it sit for 10 minutes to absorb the flavors.
3. **Grill the Chicken:** Preheat the grill to medium-high heat. Grill the chicken for 5-7 minutes on each side until fully cooked.
4. **Cook the Quinoa:** While the chicken grills, prepare 1/2 cup of quinoa according to package instructions.
5. **Steam the Broccoli:** Steam 1 cup of broccoli until tender but still vibrant green.
6. **Assemble the Plate:** Serve the grilled chicken alongside the cooked quinoa and steamed broccoli.
7. **Serve:** Enjoy immediately for a balanced, protein-rich lunch.

TIPS FOR QUICK AND SUSTAINABLE PREPARATION:

- **Make-Ahead:** Marinate the chicken the night before for quicker cooking time during lunch.
- **Batch Cooking:** Prepare extra quinoa to use in other meals throughout the week.

ADAPTATIONS FOR LONG-TERM SUCCESS:

- **Balanced Nutrition:** This meal offers a perfect balance of lean protein, healthy fats, and fiber, ensuring you stay full and satisfied.
- **Sustainability:** The recipe is versatile and can be adjusted with different herbs or vegetables for variety.

NUTRITIONAL VALUES:

Calories: 320 kcal | Protein: 1.6 oz | Carbohydrates: 1.0 oz | Fiber: 0.4 oz | Fat: 1.0 oz

TURKEY & VEGGIE LETTUCE WRAPS

PREPARATION TIME: 10 min.

COOKING TIME: 10 min.

SERVINGS: 2 servings

TARGETED INGREDIENTS:

- 4 oz ground turkey (lean protein, low in fat)
- 1/4 cup diced bell peppers (low-calorie, high in vitamins)
- 1/4 cup diced onions (adds flavor, low in calories)
- 1 Tbsp low-sodium soy sauce (adds flavor without excess sodium)
- 1 tsp olive oil (healthy fats)
- 4 large lettuce leaves (low-carb wrap alternative)
- Salt and pepper to taste (use sparingly to control sodium intake)

INSTRUCTIONS FOCUSED ON DR. NOWZARADAN'S PLAN:

1. **Cook the Turkey:** In a non-stick pan, heat 1 tsp olive oil over medium heat. Add 4 oz of ground turkey and cook until browned, about 5-7 minutes.
2. **Add Vegetables:** Add 1/4 cup diced bell peppers and 1/4 cup diced onions to the pan. Cook for an additional 3-4 minutes until the vegetables are softened.
3. **Season:** Stir in 1 Tbsp low-sodium soy sauce, and cook for 1-2 minutes to combine the flavors.
4. **Prepare the Wraps:** Lay out 4 large lettuce leaves and spoon the turkey mixture into the center of each leaf.
5. **Serve:** Fold the lettuce leaves around the filling and serve immediately.

TIPS FOR QUICK AND SUSTAINABLE PREPARATION:

- **Batch Cooking:** Prepare a larger batch of the turkey mixture to use in wraps throughout the week.
- **Make-Ahead:** Dice the vegetables ahead of time for quicker meal assembly.

ADAPTATIONS FOR LONG-TERM SUCCESS:

- **Balanced Nutrition:** These wraps offer lean protein and fiber while keeping carbs low, perfect for a light, satisfying lunch.
- **Sustainability:** The recipe is easy to prepare and can be adapted with different vegetables or proteins to keep it fresh.

NUTRITIONAL VALUES:

Calories: 240 kcal | Protein: 1.4 oz | Carbohydrates: 0.5 oz | Fiber: 0.2 oz | Fat: 0.7 oz

BALSAMIC GLAZED SALMON WITH ASPARAGUS

PREPARATION TIME: 10 min.

COOKING TIME: 15 min.

SERVINGS: 2 servings

TARGETED INGREDIENTS:

- 4 oz salmon fillet (high in protein, rich in omega-3 fatty acids)
- 1 Tbsp balsamic vinegar (adds flavor with minimal calories)
- 1 tsp honey (optional, for a touch of sweetness)
- 1 cup asparagus (fiber, low-carb)
- 1 tsp olive oil (healthy fats)
- Salt and pepper to taste (use sparingly to control sodium intake)

INSTRUCTIONS FOCUSED ON DR. NOWZARADAN'S PLAN:

1. **Prepare the Glaze:** In a small bowl, mix 1 Tbsp balsamic vinegar and 1 tsp honey if using.
2. **Cook the Salmon:** Preheat the oven to 375°F (190°C). Place the salmon fillet on a baking sheet, brush with the balsamic glaze, and season with salt and pepper. Bake for 12-15 minutes until the salmon is cooked through.
3. **Cook the Asparagus:** While the salmon bakes, heat 1 tsp olive oil in a non-stick pan over medium heat. Add 1 cup of asparagus and sauté until tender, about 5 minutes.
4. **Assemble the Plate:** Serve the salmon alongside the sautéed asparagus.
5. **Serve:** Enjoy immediately for a balanced, protein-rich lunch.

TIPS FOR QUICK AND SUSTAINABLE PREPARATION:

- **Make-Ahead:** Prepare the balsamic glaze ahead of time for quicker meal preparation.
- **Batch Cooking:** Cook extra salmon to use in salads or wraps throughout the week.

ADAPTATIONS FOR LONG-TERM SUCCESS:

- **Balanced Nutrition:** This meal provides a combination of lean protein, healthy fats, and fiber, making it both satisfying and nutritious.
- **Sustainability:** The recipe is versatile, allowing you to switch up the vegetables or protein source to keep it varied.

NUTRITIONAL VALUES:

Calories: 300 kcal | Protein: 1.5 oz | Carbohydrates: 0.5 oz | Fiber: 0.3 oz | Fat: 1.2 oz

CHICKEN & AVOCADO SALAD WITH GREEK YOGURT DRESSING

PREPARATION TIME: 10 min.
COOKING TIME: 10 min.
SERVINGS: 2 servings
TARGETED INGREDIENTS:

- 4 oz grilled chicken breast (lean protein, low in fat)
- 1/2 avocado (healthy fats, fiber)
- 2 cups mixed greens (low-calorie, rich in vitamins)
- 1/4 cup cherry tomatoes (antioxidants, low in calories)
- 2 Tbsp plain Greek yogurt (high in protein, low in fat)
- 1 Tbsp lemon juice (low-calorie flavor boost)
- Salt and pepper to taste (use sparingly to control sodium intake)

INSTRUCTIONS FOCUSED ON DR. NOWZARADAN'S PLAN:

1. **Grill the Chicken:** Season 4 oz of chicken breast with salt and pepper, then grill over medium heat for 5-7 minutes on each side until fully cooked. Let it cool slightly before slicing.
2. **Prepare the Salad Base:** In a large bowl, combine 2 cups of mixed greens and 1/4 cup cherry tomatoes.
3. **Add Healthy Fats:** Slice 1/2 avocado and add it to the salad for healthy fats that keep you satisfied.
4. **Top with Chicken:** Place the sliced grilled chicken on top of the salad.
5. **Prepare the Dressing:** In a small bowl, mix 2 Tbsp plain Greek yogurt with 1 Tbsp lemon juice. Season with salt and pepper to taste.
6. **Dress the Salad:** Drizzle the Greek yogurt dressing over the salad and toss gently to combine.
7. **Serve:** Enjoy immediately for a light, protein-rich lunch.

TIPS FOR QUICK AND SUSTAINABLE PREPARATION:

- **Advance Prep:** Grill extra chicken breast and store in the refrigerator for quick salad assembly throughout the week.

ADAPTATIONS FOR LONG-TERM SUCCESS:

- **Balanced Nutrition:** This salad offers a balance of lean protein, healthy fats, and fiber, making it a satisfying and nutritious option.
- **Sustainability:** The recipe is simple to prepare and versatile, allowing you to switch up the vegetables or dressing to keep it fresh.

NUTRITIONAL VALUES:

Calories: 340 kcal | Protein: 1.4 oz | Carbohydrates: 0.7 oz | Fiber: 0.3 oz | Fat: 1.2 oz

TOFU & VEGGIE STIR-FRY

PREPARATION TIME: 10 min.
COOKING TIME: 10 min.
SERVINGS: 2 servings
TARGETED INGREDIENTS:

- 4 oz firm tofu (plant-based protein, low in fat)
- 1/2 cup sliced bell peppers (low-calorie, high in vitamins)
- 1/2 cup broccoli florets (fiber, low-carb)

- 1 Tbsp low-sodium soy sauce (adds flavor without excess sodium)
- 1 tsp sesame oil (optional, for added flavor)
- 1/2 tsp fresh grated ginger (optional, for flavor and anti-inflammatory benefits)
- Salt and pepper to taste (use sparingly to control sodium intake)

INSTRUCTIONS FOCUSED ON DR. NOWZARADAN'S PLAN:

1. **Prepare the Tofu:** Drain and press 4 oz of firm tofu to remove excess moisture, then cut into cubes.
2. **Cook the Tofu:** In a non-stick pan, heat 1 tsp sesame oil over medium heat. Add the tofu cubes and cook until golden brown on all sides, about 5-7 minutes.
3. **Stir-Fry the Vegetables:** Add 1/2 cup sliced bell peppers and 1/2 cup broccoli florets to the pan. Stir-fry for 3-4 minutes until the vegetables are tender.
4. **Season:** Add 1 Tbsp low-sodium soy sauce and 1/2 tsp fresh grated ginger if using. Stir to combine and cook for an additional 1-2 minutes.
5. **Serve:** Enjoy immediately for a balanced, plant-based protein lunch.

TIPS FOR QUICK AND SUSTAINABLE PREPARATION:

- **Batch Cooking:** Prepare a larger portion and store in the refrigerator for a quick, reheat able lunch.
- **Make-Ahead:** Dice the tofu and vegetables ahead of time for quicker meal assembly.

ADAPTATIONS FOR LONG-TERM SUCCESS:

- **Balanced Nutrition:** This stir-fry offers a combination of plant-based protein and fiber, making it a satisfying and nutritious option.

- **Sustainability:** The recipe is versatile and can be adjusted with different vegetables or sauces to keep it varied.

NUTRITIONAL VALUES:

Calories: 270 kcal | Protein: 1.0 oz | Carbohydrates: 0.8 o | Fiber: 0.3 oz | Fat: 1.0 oz

EGG WHITE & SPINACH WRAP

PREPARATION TIME: 5 min.

COOKING TIME: 5 min.

SERVINGS: 2 servings

TARGETED INGREDIENTS:

- 6 egg whites (lean protein, low in fat)
- 1 cup fresh spinach (low-calorie, rich in iron and vitamins)
- 1 whole wheat tortilla (fiber, low in calories)
- 1/4 cup shredded low-fat cheese (optional, for flavor without excess calories)
- 1 tsp olive oil (optional, for cooking)
- Salt and pepper to taste (use sparingly to control sodium intake)

INSTRUCTIONS FOCUSED ON DR. NOWZARADAN'S PLAN:

1. **Cook the Egg Whites:** In a non-stick pan, heat 1 tsp olive oil over medium heat. Add 6 egg whites and scramble until fully cooked.
2. **Add the Spinach:** Add 1 cup fresh spinach to the pan and cook until wilted, about 2 minutes.
3. **Assemble the Wrap:** Place the egg white and spinach mixture onto a whole wheat tortilla. Sprinkle 1/4 cup shredded low-fat cheese over the top if using.
4. **Wrap and Serve:** Roll up the tortilla and serve immediately for a protein-rich, light lunch.

TIPS FOR QUICK AND SUSTAINABLE PREPARATION:

- **Make-Ahead:** Cook the egg whites and spinach ahead of time for quick assembly during lunch.

- **Batch Cooking:** Prepare extra wraps and store them in the refrigerator for a quick grab-and-go meal.

ADAPTATIONS FOR LONG-TERM SUCCESS:

- **Balanced Nutrition:** This wrap provides a combination of lean protein, fiber, and healthy fats, making it a satisfying and nutritious option.
- **Sustainability:** The recipe is simple to prepare and versatile, allowing you to switch up the vegetables or protein source to keep it fresh.

NUTRITIONAL VALUES:

Calories: 240 kcal | Protein: 1.2 oz | Carbohydrates: 1.0 oz | Fiber: 0.4 oz | Fat: 0.5 oz

GREEK YOGURT & BERRY PARFAIT

PREPARATION TIME: 5 min.
COOKING TIME: None
SERVINGS: 2 servings
TARGETED INGREDIENTS:

- 1 cup plain Greek yogurt (high in protein, low in fat)
- 1/4 cup mixed berries (low-calorie, high in antioxidants)
- 1 Tbsp chia seeds (fiber, omega-3 fatty acids)
- 1 Tbsp honey (optional, for natural sweetness)
- 1/4 tsp cinnamon (optional, for added flavor)

INSTRUCTIONS FOCUSED ON DR. NOWZARADAN'S PLAN:

1. **Layer the Ingredients:** In a glass or bowl, layer 1 cup of plain Greek yogurt, 1/4 cup mixed berries, and 1 Tbsp chia seeds.
2. **Optional Sweetness:** Drizzle 1 Tbsp honey over the top for natural sweetness if desired.
3. **Add Flavor:** Sprinkle with 1/4 tsp cinnamon for added flavor and potential blood sugar regulation.

4. **Serve:** Enjoy immediately for a light, protein-rich lunch.

TIPS FOR QUICK AND SUSTAINABLE PREPARATION:

- **Make-Ahead:** Assemble the parfait the night before for a quick grab-and-go lunch.
- **Batch Cooking:** Prepare multiple parfaits and store them in the refrigerator for easy access throughout the week.

ADAPTATIONS FOR LONG-TERM SUCCESS:

- **Balanced Nutrition:** This parfait provides a mix of protein, fiber, and healthy fats, making it a light and satisfying option.
- **Sustainability:** The recipe is easy to prepare and versatile, allowing you to switch up the fruits or add nuts for variety.

NUTRITIONAL VALUES:

Calories: 220 kcal | Protein: 1.1 oz | Carbohydrates: 1.0 oz | Fiber: 0.3 oz | Fat: 0.4 oz

8.3 HEALTHY LUNCHES ON THE GO

TURKEY & AVOCADO WRAP

PREPARATION TIME: 5 min.
COOKING TIME: None
SERVINGS: 2 servings
TARGETED INGREDIENTS:

- 4 oz sliced turkey breast (lean protein, low in fat)
- 1/2 avocado (healthy fats, fiber)
- 1 whole wheat tortilla (fiber, low in calories)
- 1/4 cup mixed greens (low-calorie, rich in vitamins)
- 1 Tbsp hummus (optional, for added flavor and fiber)
- Salt and pepper to taste (use sparingly to control sodium intake)

INSTRUCTIONS FOCUSED ON DR. NOWZARADAN'S PLAN:

1. **Assemble the Wrap:** Lay out the whole wheat tortilla and spread 1 Tbsp of hummus if using.
2. **Add the Ingredients:** Layer 4 oz of sliced turkey breast, 1/2 sliced avocado, and 1/4 cup of mixed greens on the tortilla.
3. **Season & Wrap:** Season with salt and pepper to taste, then roll up the tortilla tightly to create a wrap.
4. **Serve or Pack:** Cut in half if desired, and either serve immediately or wrap tightly in foil for a portable lunch.

TIPS FOR QUICK AND SUSTAINABLE PREPARATION:

- **Make-Ahead:** Prepare the wrap the night before and store in the refrigerator for a quick grab-and-go lunch.
- **Batch Cooking:** Make multiple wraps at once for easy access throughout the week.

ADAPTATIONS FOR LONG-TERM SUCCESS:

- **Balanced Nutrition:** This wrap provides lean protein, healthy fats, and fiber, keeping you satisfied and energized without weighing you down.
- **Sustainability:** Simple to prepare and versatile, allowing you to switch up the fillings or add different vegetables to keep it varied.

NUTRITIONAL VALUES:

Calories: 350 kcal | Protein: 1.4 oz | Carbohydrates: 1.0 oz | Fiber: 0.5 oz | Fat: 1.2 oz

CHICKPEA SALAD JAR

PREPARATION TIME: 10 min.

COOKING TIME: None

SERVINGS: 2 servings

TARGETED INGREDIENTS:

- 1/2 cup canned chickpeas (drained and rinsed; plant-based protein, high in fiber)
- 1/4 cup diced cucumber (hydrating, low in calories)
- 1/4 cup cherry tomatoes (antioxidants, low in calories)
- 2 Tbsp crumbled feta cheese (optional, adds flavor without excessive calories)
- 1 Tbsp olive oil (healthy fats)
- 1 Tbsp lemon juice (low-calorie flavor boost)
- Salt and pepper to taste (use sparingly to control sodium intake)

INSTRUCTIONS FOCUSED ON DR. NOWZARADAN'S PLAN:

1. **Layer the Ingredients:** In a mason jar or portable container, layer the following: 1/2 cup chickpeas, 1/4 cup diced cucumber, 1/4 cup cherry tomatoes, and 2 Tbsp crumbled feta cheese if using.
2. **Add the Dressing:** Drizzle 1 Tbsp olive oil and 1 Tbsp lemon juice over the top.
3. **Season & Serve:** Season with salt and pepper to taste. Close the jar tightly and shake before eating to mix the ingredients.
4. **Store:** Keep in the refrigerator until ready to eat, making it an ideal portable lunch option.

TIPS FOR QUICK AND SUSTAINABLE PREPARATION:

- **Batch Cooking:** Prepare several salad jars at once and store them in the refrigerator for easy lunches throughout the week.
- **Make-Ahead:** These salad jars can be made the night before and stored for a quick, portable meal.

ADAPTATIONS FOR LONG-TERM SUCCESS:

- **Balanced Nutrition:** This chickpea salad jar offers a mix of plant-based protein, healthy fats, and fiber, making it both satisfying and nutritious.
- **Sustainability:** The recipe is easy to prepare and can be customized with different vegetables or dressings to keep it exciting.

NUTRITIONAL VALUES:

Calories: 280 kcal | Protein: 1.0 oz | Carbohydrates: 1.2 oz | Fiber: 0.6 oz | Fat: 0.9 oz

GRILLED CHICKEN & QUINOA BOWL

PREPARATION TIME: 10 min.
COOKING TIME: 15 min.
SERVINGS: 2 servings
TARGETED INGREDIENTS:

- 4 oz grilled chicken breast (lean protein, low in fat)
- 1/2 cup cooked quinoa (complete protein, fiber-rich)
- 1/2 cup steamed broccoli (fiber, low-carb)
- 1/4 cup diced bell peppers (adds color, low in calories)
- 1 Tbsp olive oil (healthy fats)
- Salt and pepper to taste (use sparingly to control sodium intake)

INSTRUCTIONS FOCUSED ON DR. NOWZARADAN'S PLAN:

1. **Cook the Quinoa:** Prepare 1/2 cup of quinoa according to package instructions and allow it to cool slightly.
2. **Grill the Chicken:** Season 4 oz of chicken breast with salt and pepper, then grill over medium heat for 5-7 minutes on each side until fully cooked.
3. **Assemble the Bowl:** In a portable container, layer the following: cooked quinoa, grilled chicken (sliced), 1/2 cup steamed broccoli, and 1/4 cup diced bell peppers.
4. **Add Dressing:** Drizzle 1 Tbsp olive oil over the bowl and season with salt and pepper to taste.
5. **Serve or Pack:** Enjoy immediately or pack for a balanced, protein-rich lunch on the go.

TIPS FOR QUICK AND SUSTAINABLE PREPARATION:

- **Make-Ahead:** Prepare the quinoa and chicken the night before for quicker meal assembly.
- **Batch Cooking:** Cook extra quinoa and chicken for use in other meals throughout the week.

ADAPTATIONS FOR LONG-TERM SUCCESS:

- **Balanced Nutrition:** This bowl provides a perfect balance of lean protein, healthy fats, and fiber, ensuring a satisfying and nutritious lunch.
- **Sustainability:** The recipe is versatile, allowing you to switch up the vegetables or protein source to keep it varied.

NUTRITIONAL VALUES:

Calories: 350 kcal | Protein: 1.6 oz | Carbohydrates: 1.0 oz | Fiber: 0.4 oz | Fat: 1.0 oz

TOFU & VEGGIE NOODLE SALAD

PREPARATION TIME: 10 min.
COOKING TIME: 5 min.
SERVINGS: 2 servings
TARGETED INGREDIENTS:

- 4 oz firm tofu (plant-based protein, low in fat)
- 1 cup spiralized zucchini (low-carb, high in fiber)
- 1/4 cup shredded carrots (adds color, low in calories)
- 1 Tbsp low-sodium soy sauce (adds flavor without excess sodium)

- 1 Tbsp sesame oil (optional, for added flavor)
- 1 tsp sesame seeds (healthy fats, adds texture)
- Salt and pepper to taste (use sparingly to control sodium intake)

INSTRUCTIONS FOCUSED ON DR. NOWZARADAN'S PLAN:

1. **Prepare the Tofu:** Drain and press 4 oz of firm tofu to remove excess moisture, then cut into cubes.
2. **Cook the Tofu:** In a non-stick pan, sauté the tofu cubes over medium heat until golden brown on all sides, about 5-7 minutes. Let it cool slightly.
3. **Assemble the Salad:** In a portable container, combine the tofu, 1 cup spiralized zucchini, and 1/4 cup shredded carrots.
4. **Add Dressing:** Drizzle 1 Tbsp low-sodium soy sauce and 1 Tbsp sesame oil over the salad. Toss gently to combine.
5. **Serve or Pack:** Sprinkle with 1 tsp sesame seeds, season with salt and pepper to taste, and either serve immediately or pack for a light, plant-based lunch.

TIPS FOR QUICK AND SUSTAINABLE PREPARATION:

- **Make-Ahead:** Prepare the tofu and vegetables ahead of time for quicker assembly during lunch.
- **Batch Cooking:** Cook extra tofu to use in other meals throughout the week.

ADAPTATIONS FOR LONG-TERM SUCCESS:

- **Balanced Nutrition:** This noodle salad offers a combination of plant-based protein and fiber, making it a satisfying and nutritious option.
- **Sustainability:** The recipe is versatile and can be adjusted with different vegetables or dressings to keep it varied.

NUTRITIONAL VALUES:

Calories: 280 kcal | Protein: 1.0 oz | Carbohydrates: 0.7 oz | Fiber: 0.4 oz | Fat: 1.0 oz

EGG SALAD LETTUCE CUPS

PREPARATION TIME: 10 min.

COOKING TIME: None

SERVINGS: 2 servings

TARGETED INGREDIENTS:

- 6 hard-boiled egg whites (lean protein, low in fat)
- 1 Tbsp plain Greek yogurt (high in protein, low in fat)
- 1 tsp Dijon mustard (adds flavor with minimal calories)
- 1/4 cup diced celery (adds crunch, low in calories)
- 1 Tbsp chopped chives (optional, for added flavor)
- 4 large lettuce leaves (low-carb wrap alternative)
- Salt and pepper to taste (use sparingly to control sodium intake)

INSTRUCTIONS FOCUSED ON DR. NOWZARADAN'S PLAN:

1. **Prepare the Egg Salad:** Chop 6 hard-boiled egg whites and place them in a bowl. Add 1 Tbsp plain Greek yogurt, 1 tsp Dijon mustard, and 1/4 cup diced celery. Mix well to combine.
2. **Season:** Stir in 1 Tbsp chopped chives if using, and season with salt and pepper to taste.
3. **Assemble the Lettuce Cups:** Spoon the egg salad into 4 large lettuce leaves.
4. **Serve or Pack:** Fold the lettuce leaves around the egg salad and serve immediately or pack for a portable, protein-rich lunch.

TIPS FOR QUICK AND SUSTAINABLE PREPARATION:

- **Make-Ahead:** Prepare the egg salad the night before for a quick, ready-to-eat lunch.

- **Batch Cooking:** Prepare extra egg salad to use in sandwiches or wraps throughout the week.

ADAPTATIONS FOR LONG-TERM SUCCESS:

- **Balanced Nutrition:** These lettuce cups provide lean protein and fiber while keeping carbs low, making them a light and satisfying lunch option.
- **Sustainability:** The recipe is simple to prepare and versatile, allowing you to switch up the fillings or add different vegetables to keep it fresh.

NUTRITIONAL VALUES:

Calories: 220 kcal | Protein: 1.3 oz | Carbohydrates: 0.3 oz | Fiber: 0.2 oz | Fat: 0.5 oz

LENTIL & VEGETABLE SOUP

PREPARATION TIME: 10 min.
COOKING TIME: 20 min.
SERVINGS: 2 servings
TARGETED INGREDIENTS:

- 1/2 cup cooked lentils (plant-based protein, high in fiber)
- 1/2 cup diced carrots (adds sweetness, low in calories)
- 1/2 cup diced celery (adds crunch, low in calories)
- 1/4 cup diced onions (adds flavor, low in calories)
- 2 cups low-sodium vegetable broth (base for the soup)
- 1 tsp olive oil (healthy fats)
- 1 tsp Italian seasoning (optional, for added flavor)
- Salt and pepper to taste (use sparingly to control sodium intake)

INSTRUCTIONS FOCUSED ON DR. NOWZARADAN'S PLAN:

1. **Prepare the Vegetables:** In a large pot, heat 1 tsp olive oil over medium heat. Add 1/4 cup diced onions, 1/2 cup diced carrots, and 1/2 cup diced celery. Cook until softened, about 5 minutes.
2. **Add the Lentils:** Stir in 1/2 cup cooked lentils and 1 tsp Italian seasoning if using.
3. **Add Broth & Simmer:** Pour in 2 cups of low-sodium vegetable broth and bring to a boil. Reduce heat and simmer for 15 minutes to allow the flavors to meld.
4. **Serve or Store:** Season with salt and pepper to taste, and serve immediately, or store in the refrigerator for a quick, reheat able lunch.

TIPS FOR QUICK AND SUSTAINABLE PREPARATION:

- **Batch Cooking:** Make a larger batch and store portions in the refrigerator or freezer for easy meals throughout the week.
- **Make-Ahead:** Prepare the soup ahead of time and reheat when ready to eat.

ADAPTATIONS FOR LONG-TERM SUCCESS:

- **Balanced Nutrition:** This soup offers a combination of plant-based protein and fiber, making it both satisfying and nutritious.
- **Sustainability:** The recipe is easy to prepare and versatile, allowing you to adjust the vegetables or seasoning to keep it fresh.

NUTRITIONAL VALUES:

Calories: 230 kcal | Protein: 1.0 oz | Carbohydrates: 1.2 oz | Fiber: 0.6 oz | Fat: 0.5 oz

CHAPTER 9: DINNER RECIPES FOR A SATISFYING END TO YOUR DAY

9.1 HEARTY AND HEALTHY DINNERS

BAKED SALMON WITH QUINOA AND SPINACH

PREPARATION TIME: 10 min.

COOKING TIME: 20 min.

SERVINGS: 2 servings

TARGETED INGREDIENTS:

- 4 oz salmon fillet (high in protein, rich in omega-3 fatty acids)
- 1/2 cup cooked quinoa (complete protein, fiber-rich)
- 1 cup fresh spinach (low-calorie, rich in iron and vitamins)
- 1 tsp olive oil (healthy fats)
- 1 Tbsp lemon juice (low-calorie flavor boost)
- Salt and pepper to taste (use sparingly to control sodium intake)

INSTRUCTIONS FOCUSED ON DR. NOWZARADAN'S PLAN:

1. **Prepare the Salmon:** Preheat the oven to 375°F (190°C). Place the salmon fillet on a baking sheet lined with parchment paper. Drizzle with 1 tsp olive oil and 1 Tbsp lemon juice, and season with salt and pepper.

2. **Bake the Salmon:** Bake in the preheated oven for 15-20 minutes, until the salmon is fully cooked and flakes easily with a fork.

3. **Cook the Quinoa:** While the salmon is baking, prepare 1/2 cup quinoa according to package instructions.

4. **Sauté the Spinach:** In a non-stick pan, sauté the spinach over medium heat until wilted, about 2-3 minutes.

5. **Assemble the Plate:** Serve the baked salmon alongside the cooked quinoa and sautéed spinach.

6. **Serve:** Enjoy immediately for a well-balanced, satisfying dinner.

TIPS FOR QUICK AND SUSTAINABLE PREPARATION:

- **Make-Ahead:** Cook extra quinoa and store it in the refrigerator for use in other meals throughout the week.
- **Batch Cooking:** Prepare additional portions of salmon to have ready-made meals for the next day.

ADAPTATIONS FOR LONG-TERM SUCCESS:

- **Balanced Nutrition:** This meal provides a combination of lean protein, healthy fats, and fiber-rich carbohydrates, ensuring a satisfying and nutritious dinner.
- **Sustainability:** Versatile and easy to prepare, this recipe allows for substitutions with different greens or grains to keep it varied.

NUTRITIONAL VALUES:

Calories: 320 kcal | Protein: 1.6 oz | Carbohydrates: 1.0 oz | Fiber: 0.4 oz | Fat: 1.2 oz

LEMON HERB GRILLED CHICKEN WITH ROASTED VEGETABLES

PREPARATION TIME: 10 min.
COOKING TIME: 25 min.
SERVINGS: 2 servings
TARGETED INGREDIENTS:

- 4 oz chicken breast (lean protein, low in fat)
- 1 Tbsp olive oil (healthy fats)
- 1 Tbsp lemon juice (low-calorie flavor boost)
- 1 tsp fresh chopped herbs (thyme, rosemary, or parsley)
- 1 cup broccoli florets (fiber, low-carb)
- 1/2 cup sliced bell peppers (rich in vitamins, low in calories)
- 1/2 cup zucchini slices (fiber, low-carb)
- Salt and pepper to taste (use sparingly to control sodium intake)

INSTRUCTIONS FOCUSED ON DR. NOWZARADAN'S PLAN:

1. **Marinate the Chicken:** In a small bowl, mix 1 Tbsp olive oil, 1 Tbsp lemon juice, and 1 tsp fresh chopped herbs. Coat the chicken breast in the marinade and let it sit for 10 minutes.
2. **Prepare the Vegetables:** While the chicken marinates, preheat the oven to 375°F (190°C). Arrange the broccoli, bell peppers, and zucchini on a baking sheet. Drizzle with a small amount of olive oil and season with salt and pepper.
3. **Roast the Vegetables:** Roast the vegetables in the preheated oven for 20 minutes, or until tender and slightly browned.
4. **Grill the Chicken:** While the vegetables are roasting, heat a grill pan over medium-high heat. Grill the chicken for 5-7 minutes on each side until fully cooked.
5. **Serve:** Plate the grilled chicken with the roasted vegetables. Enjoy a balanced, hearty dinner.

TIPS FOR QUICK AND SUSTAINABLE PREPARATION:

- **Advance Prep:** Marinate the chicken earlier in the day or the night before for even more flavor and quicker cooking time.
- **Batch Cooking:** Roast extra vegetables and cook additional chicken breasts to have ready-made meals for the next day.

ADAPTATIONS FOR LONG-TERM SUCCESS:

- **Balanced Nutrition:** This recipe offers a perfect balance of lean protein, healthy fats, and fiber-rich vegetables, adhering to Dr. Nowzaradan's principles of a nutritious, calorie-conscious diet.
- **Sustainability:** Simple and adaptable, this recipe allows for easy substitutions with different herbs or vegetables to keep meals varied and exciting.

NUTRITIONAL VALUES:

Calories: 280 kcal | Protein: 1.4 oz | Carbohydrates: 0.8 oz | Fiber: 0.4 oz | Fat: 0.9 oz

TURKEY MEATBALLS WITH ZUCCHINI NOODLES

PREPARATION TIME: 15 min.
COOKING TIME: 25 min.
SERVINGS: 2 servings
TARGETED INGREDIENTS:

- 4 oz ground turkey (lean protein, low in fat)
- 1/4 cup grated Parmesan cheese (adds flavor without excess calories)
- 1 egg white (binds the meatballs, adds lean protein)
- 1/2 tsp garlic powder (flavor without calories)
- 1/2 tsp Italian seasoning (optional, for flavor)
- 1 cup zucchini noodles (low-carb, high in fiber)

- 1 cup marinara sauce (low-sugar, low-sodium)
- Salt and pepper to taste (use sparingly to control sodium intake)

INSTRUCTIONS FOCUSED ON DR. NOWZARADAN'S PLAN:

1. **Prepare the Meatballs:** Preheat the oven to 375°F (190°C). In a bowl, mix 4 oz ground turkey with 1/4 cup grated Parmesan cheese, 1 egg white, 1/2 tsp garlic powder, and 1/2 tsp Italian seasoning. Season with salt and pepper.

2. **Form the Meatballs:** Roll the turkey mixture into small meatballs, about 1 inch in diameter, and place them on a baking sheet lined with parchment paper.

3. **Bake the Meatballs:** Bake in the preheated oven for 20-25 minutes, until fully cooked and golden brown.

4. **Cook the Zucchini Noodles:** While the meatballs are baking, sauté 1 cup zucchini noodles in a non-stick pan over medium heat for 2-3 minutes, until tender.

5. **Warm the Marinara Sauce:** In a small saucepan, heat 1 cup marinara sauce over low heat until warmed through.

6. **Assemble the Dish:** Serve the turkey meatballs over the zucchini noodles and top with marinara sauce.

7. **Serve:** Enjoy immediately for a filling, low-carb dinner.

TIPS FOR QUICK AND SUSTAINABLE PREPARATION:

- **Make-Ahead:** Prepare the meatballs ahead of time and freeze for quick dinners during the week.
- **Batch Cooking:** Double the recipe and store extra portions for ready-made meals.

ADAPTATIONS FOR LONG-TERM SUCCESS:

- **Balanced Nutrition:** This dish provides a satisfying combination of lean protein, healthy fats, and fiber, making it a nutritious and filling dinner option.
- **Sustainability:** Easy to prepare and versatile, this recipe allows for variations with different proteins or vegetable noodles to keep it exciting.

NUTRITIONAL VALUES:

Calories: 300 kcal | Protein: 1.4 oz | Carbohydrates: 0.8 oz | Fiber: 0.3 oz | Fat: 0.9 oz

QUINOA STUFFED BELL PEPPERS

PREPARATION TIME: 15 min.

COOKING TIME: 30 min.

SERVINGS: 2 servings

TARGETED INGREDIENTS:

- 2 large bell peppers (fiber, low-calorie)
- 1/2 cup cooked quinoa (complete protein, fiber-rich)
- 4 oz ground turkey or lean beef (lean protein, low in fat)
- 1/4 cup diced tomatoes (adds flavor, low in calories)
- 1/4 cup black beans (adds fiber and protein)
- 1 tsp olive oil (healthy fats)
- 1 tsp cumin (optional, for added flavor)
- Salt and pepper to taste (use sparingly to control sodium intake)

INSTRUCTIONS FOCUSED ON DR. NOWZARADAN'S PLAN:

1. **Prepare the Peppers:** Preheat the oven to 375°F (190°C). Cut the tops off the bell peppers and remove the seeds. Set aside.

2. **Cook the Filling:** In a non-stick pan, heat 1 tsp olive oil over medium heat. Add 4 oz ground turkey or lean beef and

9.2 LOW-CALORIE COMFORT FOODS

CAULIFLOWER MASH WITH TURKEY MEATLOAF

PREPARATION TIME: 15 min.
COOKING TIME: 40 min.
SERVINGS: 2 servings
TARGETED INGREDIENTS:

- 8 oz ground turkey (lean protein, low in fat)
- 1/4 cup whole wheat breadcrumbs (fiber, adds texture)
- 1 egg white (binds the meatloaf, adds lean protein)
- 1/4 cup diced onion (flavor, low in calories)
- 1 tsp garlic powder (flavor without calories)
- 1 tsp Italian seasoning (optional, for flavor)
- 1 head of cauliflower, chopped (low-carb, high in fiber)
- 1 Tbsp low-fat milk (adds creaminess without excess calories)
- Salt and pepper to taste (use sparingly to control sodium intake)

INSTRUCTIONS FOCUSED ON DR. NOWZARADAN'S PLAN:

1. **Prepare the Meatloaf:** Preheat the oven to 375°F (190°C). In a large bowl, mix 8 oz ground turkey, 1/4 cup whole wheat breadcrumbs, 1 egg white, 1/4 cup diced onion, 1 tsp garlic powder, and 1 tsp Italian seasoning. Season with salt and pepper.
2. **Shape and Bake:** Form the mixture into a loaf shape and place it in a small baking dish. Bake for 35-40 minutes, or until the internal temperature reaches 165°F (74°C).
3. **Cook the Cauliflower:** While the meatloaf is baking, steam the chopped cauliflower until tender, about 10 minutes.
4. **Mash the Cauliflower:** Once tender, transfer the cauliflower to a food processor. Add 1 Tbsp low-fat milk, salt, and pepper, and blend until smooth and creamy.

5. **Serve:** Slice the meatloaf and serve it alongside the cauliflower mash for a comforting, low-calorie dinner.

TIPS FOR QUICK AND SUSTAINABLE PREPARATION:

- **Batch Cooking:** Double the meatloaf recipe and freeze individual portions for quick dinners.
- **Make-Ahead:** Prepare the cauliflower mash ahead of time and reheat when ready to serve.

ADAPTATIONS FOR LONG-TERM SUCCESS:

- **Balanced Nutrition:** This meal combines lean protein with a low-carb vegetable mash, keeping calories low while providing essential nutrients.
- **Sustainability:** Simple and versatile, this recipe allows for easy substitutions, like using ground chicken or beef.

NUTRITIONAL VALUES:

Calories: 260 kcal | Protein: 1.6 oz | Carbohydrates: 0.8 oz | Fiber: 0.4 oz | Fat: 0.7 oz

ZUCCHINI LASAGNA

PREPARATION TIME: 20 min.
COOKING TIME: 30 min.
SERVINGS: 2 servings
TARGETED INGREDIENTS:

- 2 large zucchinis, sliced thinly (low-carb, high in fiber)
- 8 oz ground turkey or lean beef (lean protein, low in fat)
- 1 cup marinara sauce (low-sodium, low-sugar)
- 1/2 cup part-skim ricotta cheese (adds creaminess without excess calories)
- 1/4 cup shredded low-fat mozzarella cheese (optional, for flavor)
- 1 tsp Italian seasoning (optional, for flavor)
- Salt and pepper to taste (use sparingly to control sodium intake)

INSTRUCTIONS FOCUSED ON DR. NOWZARADAN'S PLAN:

1. **Prepare the Zucchini:** Preheat the oven to 375°F (190°C). Slice the zucchinis lengthwise into thin strips and set them aside.

2. **Cook the Meat:** In a non-stick pan, cook 8 oz of ground turkey or lean beef over medium heat until browned. Drain any excess fat, then add 1 cup of marinara sauce and 1 tsp Italian seasoning. Simmer for 5 minutes.

3. **Assemble the Lasagna:** In a baking dish, layer the zucchini slices, meat sauce, and dollops of ricotta cheese. Repeat the layers until all ingredients are used, finishing with a layer of zucchini topped with shredded mozzarella cheese.

4. **Bake:** Cover the dish with foil and bake for 25 minutes. Remove the foil and bake for an additional 5 minutes, or until the cheese is bubbly and golden.

5. **Serve:** Let the lasagna cool slightly before slicing and serving.

TIPS FOR QUICK AND SUSTAINABLE PREPARATION:

- **Advance Prep:** Slice the zucchini and cook the meat sauce ahead of time for quicker assembly.

- **Batch Cooking:** Prepare and freeze individual portions for easy weeknight dinners.

ADAPTATIONS FOR LONG-TERM SUCCESS:

- **Balanced Nutrition:** This lasagna is low in carbs and high in protein, making it a satisfying yet lighter comfort food option.

- **Sustainability:** The recipe is versatile, allowing for different fillings or the addition of vegetables like spinach or mushrooms.

NUTRITIONAL VALUES:

Calories: 300 kcal | Protein: 1.8 oz | Carbohydrates: 0.7 oz | Fiber: 0.4 oz | Fat: 0.9 oz

SPAGHETTI SQUASH WITH TURKEY BOLOGNESE

PREPARATION TIME: 15 min.

COOKING TIME: 40 min.

SERVINGS: 2 servings

TARGETED INGREDIENTS:

- 1 medium spaghetti squash (low-carb, high in fiber)
- 8 oz ground turkey (lean protein, low in fat)
- 1 cup marinara sauce (low-sodium, low-sugar)
- 1/4 cup diced onion (flavor, low in calories)
- 1 tsp garlic powder (flavor without calories)
- 1 tsp olive oil (healthy fats)
- Salt and pepper to taste (use sparingly to control sodium intake)

INSTRUCTIONS FOCUSED ON DR. NOWZARADAN'S PLAN:

1. **Prepare the Spaghetti Squash:** Preheat the oven to 375°F (190°C). Cut the spaghetti squash in half lengthwise and remove the seeds. Drizzle with 1 tsp olive oil and place cut side down on a baking sheet. Roast for 35-40 minutes, or until the flesh is tender.

2. **Cook the Bolognese:** While the squash is roasting, cook 8 oz of ground turkey in a non-stick pan over medium heat until browned. Add 1/4 cup diced onion and 1 tsp garlic powder, and cook until the onion is translucent. Stir in 1 cup marinara sauce and simmer for 10 minutes.

3. **Assemble the Dish:** Once the squash is cooked, use a fork to scrape the flesh into strands resembling spaghetti. Top with the turkey Bolognese sauce.

4. **Serve:** Enjoy immediately for a comforting, low-carb dinner.

TIPS FOR QUICK AND SUSTAINABLE PREPARATION:

- **Make-Ahead:** Cook the spaghetti squash ahead of time and store in the refrigerator for quick assembly later.
- **Batch Cooking:** Prepare extra Bolognese sauce and freeze for future meals.

ADAPTATIONS FOR LONG-TERM SUCCESS:

- **Balanced Nutrition:** This dish provides a satisfying combination of lean protein and low-carb vegetables, adhering to Dr. Nowzaradan's principles.
- **Sustainability:** Simple and versatile, this recipe allows for easy modifications, such as adding mushrooms or using ground chicken instead of turkey.

NUTRITIONAL VALUES:

Calories: 280 kcal | Protein: 1.6 oz | Carbohydrates: 1.0 oz | Fiber: 0.5 oz | Fat: 0.8 oz

---

SHEPHERD'S PIE WITH CAULIFLOWER TOPPING

PREPARATION TIME: 20 min.
COOKING TIME: 30 min.
SERVINGS: 2 servings
TARGETED INGREDIENTS:

- 8 oz lean ground beef or turkey (lean protein, low in fat)
- 1 cup frozen mixed vegetables (carrots, peas, corn)
- 1 cup low-sodium beef or chicken broth (flavorful base)
- 1 Tbsp tomato paste (adds depth of flavor)
- 1 head of cauliflower, chopped (low-carb, high in fiber)
- 1 Tbsp low-fat milk (adds creaminess without excess calories)
- Salt and pepper to taste (use sparingly to control sodium intake)

INSTRUCTIONS FOCUSED ON DR. NOWZARADAN'S PLAN:

1. **Cook the Meat:** Preheat the oven to 375°F (190°C). In a non-stick pan, cook 8 oz of lean ground beef or turkey over medium heat until browned. Drain any excess fat.
2. **Add Vegetables:** Stir in 1 cup frozen mixed vegetables, 1 Tbsp tomato paste, and 1 cup low-sodium broth. Simmer for 5-10 minutes until the vegetables are tender and the mixture has thickened slightly.
3. **Prepare the Cauliflower Topping:** While the meat is cooking, steam the chopped cauliflower until tender, about 10 minutes. Mash with 1 Tbsp low-fat milk, salt, and pepper until smooth.
4. **Assemble the Shepherd's Pie:** Transfer the meat and vegetable mixture to a baking dish. Spread the cauliflower mash evenly over the top.
5. **Bake:** Bake in the preheated oven for 20 minutes, or until the top is lightly browned.
6. **Serve:** Enjoy a warm, comforting, and low-calorie dinner.

TIPS FOR QUICK AND SUSTAINABLE PREPARATION:

- **Make-Ahead:** Prepare the meat and vegetable filling ahead of time and store in the refrigerator. Top with cauliflower mash and bake when ready to serve.
- **Batch Cooking:** Double the recipe and freeze individual portions for quick meals.

ADAPTATIONS FOR LONG-TERM SUCCESS:

- **Balanced Nutrition:** This shepherd's pie is low in carbs and high in protein, making it a filling yet lighter comfort food option.
- **Sustainability:** Versatile and easy to prepare, this recipe allows for substitutions, like using sweet potatoes or different vegetables.

NUTRITIONAL VALUES:

Calories: 320 kcal | Protein: 1.7 oz | Carbohydrates: 0.9 oz | Fiber: 0.5 oz | Fat: 0.9 oz

9.3 VEGETARIAN AND PLANT-BASED DINNER OPTIONS

STUFFED BELL PEPPERS WITH QUINOA AND BLACK BEANS

PREPARATION TIME: 15 min.

COOKING TIME: 30 min.

SERVINGS: 2 servings

TARGETED INGREDIENTS:

- 2 large bell peppers (low in calories, high in fiber)
- 1/2 cup cooked quinoa (complete protein, rich in fiber)
- 1/2 cup black beans (plant-based protein, high in fiber)
- 1/4 cup diced tomatoes (adds flavor, low in calories)
- 1/4 cup corn kernels (optional, adds sweetness and fiber)
- 1 tsp cumin (optional, for flavor)
- 1 tsp olive oil (healthy fats)
- Salt and pepper to taste (use sparingly to control sodium intake)

INSTRUCTIONS FOCUSED ON DR. NOWZARADAN'S PLAN:

1. **Prepare the Peppers:** Preheat the oven to 375°F (190°C). Cut the tops off the bell peppers and remove the seeds. Set aside.
2. **Cook the Filling:** In a non-stick pan, heat 1 tsp olive oil over medium heat. Add 1/2 cup cooked quinoa, 1/2 cup black beans, 1/4 cup diced tomatoes, and 1/4 cup corn kernels if using. Stir in 1 tsp cumin, and season with salt and pepper. Cook for 5 minutes to combine flavors.
3. **Stuff the Peppers:** Spoon the quinoa mixture into the hollowed bell peppers, filling them to the top.
4. **Bake:** Place the stuffed peppers in a baking dish, cover with foil, and bake for 25-30 minutes, until the peppers are tender.
5. **Serve:** Enjoy immediately for a hearty, plant-based dinner.

TIPS FOR QUICK AND SUSTAINABLE PREPARATION:

- **Make-Ahead:** Prepare the quinoa and filling the night before to save time on busy evenings.
- **Batch Cooking:** Double the recipe and freeze individual stuffed peppers for quick, ready-to-eat meals.

ADAPTATIONS FOR LONG-TERM SUCCESS:

- **Balanced Nutrition:** This recipe provides a combination of plant-based protein, fiber, and essential nutrients, making it a well-rounded, satisfying meal.
- **Sustainability:** Versatile and easy to prepare, this dish allows for various fillings or the addition of different vegetables to keep meals exciting.

NUTRITIONAL VALUES:

Calories: 280 kcal | Protein: 1.1 oz | Carbohydrates: 1.4 oz | Fiber: 0.5 oz | Fat: 0.6 oz

LENTIL AND VEGETABLE STIR-FRY

PREPARATION TIME: 10 min.

COOKING TIME: 20 min.

SERVINGS: 2 servings

TARGETED INGREDIENTS:

- 1 cup cooked lentils (high in protein and fiber)
- 1/2 cup broccoli florets (low in calories, high in fiber)
- 1/2 cup sliced bell peppers (rich in vitamins, low in calories)

- 1/2 cup sliced carrots (adds sweetness, high in fiber)
- 1 Tbsp soy sauce (low-sodium, for flavor)
- 1 tsp olive oil (healthy fats)
- 1 tsp ginger, minced (optional, for flavor)
- Salt and pepper to taste (use sparingly to control sodium intake)

INSTRUCTIONS FOCUSED ON DR. NOWZARADAN'S PLAN:

1. **Cook the Vegetables:** In a non-stick pan, heat 1 tsp olive oil over medium heat. Add 1/2 cup broccoli, 1/2 cup bell peppers, and 1/2 cup carrots. Cook for 5-7 minutes until the vegetables are tender.
2. **Add the Lentils:** Stir in 1 cup cooked lentils and 1 tsp minced ginger. Add 1 Tbsp soy sauce and cook for another 5 minutes, allowing the flavors to meld together.
3. **Serve:** Plate the stir-fry and enjoy immediately for a quick, nutritious dinner.

TIPS FOR QUICK AND SUSTAINABLE PREPARATION:

- **Make-Ahead:** Cook the lentils ahead of time and store them in the refrigerator for quick meals.
- **Batch Cooking:** Double the recipe and store leftovers for easy lunches or dinners.

ADAPTATIONS FOR LONG-TERM SUCCESS:

- **Balanced Nutrition:** This stir-fry is packed with plant-based protein and a variety of vegetables, making it a filling and nutrient-dense option.
- **Sustainability:** The recipe is highly adaptable, allowing you to use whatever vegetables you have on hand, making it a great way to reduce food waste.

NUTRITIONAL VALUES:

Calories: 250 kcal | Protein: 1.2 oz | Carbohydrates: 1.3 oz | Fiber: 0.7 oz | Fat: 0.5 oz

EGGPLANT AND CHICKPEA STEW

PREPARATION TIME: 15 min.

COOKING TIME: 30 min.

SERVINGS: 2 servings

TARGETED INGREDIENTS:

- 1 medium eggplant, cubed (low in calories, high in fiber)
- 1 cup cooked chickpeas (plant-based protein, high in fiber)
- 1/2 cup diced tomatoes (adds flavor, low in calories)
- 1/4 cup diced onion (flavor, low in calories)
- 1 clove garlic, minced (flavor without calories)
- 1 tsp cumin (optional, for flavor)
- 1 tsp olive oil (healthy fats)
- Salt and pepper to taste (use sparingly to control sodium intake)

INSTRUCTIONS FOCUSED ON DR. NOWZARADAN'S PLAN:

1. **Cook the Vegetables:** In a large pot, heat 1 tsp olive oil over medium heat. Add 1/4 cup diced onion and 1 minced garlic clove, cooking until translucent.
2. **Add the Eggplant:** Stir in the cubed eggplant and 1 tsp cumin. Cook for 5-7 minutes until the eggplant begins to soften.
3. **Simmer the Stew:** Add 1/2 cup diced tomatoes and 1 cup cooked chickpeas. Reduce heat to low and simmer for 20 minutes, allowing the flavors to meld.
4. **Serve:** Ladle the stew into bowls and enjoy as a hearty, plant-based dinner.

TIPS FOR QUICK AND SUSTAINABLE PREPARATION:

- **Batch Cooking:** Make a large batch of stew and freeze individual portions for easy dinners.
- **Advance Prep:** Chop the vegetables ahead of time for quicker assembly.

ADAPTATIONS FOR LONG-TERM SUCCESS:

- **Balanced Nutrition:** This stew offers a combination of plant-based protein and fiber, ensuring a satisfying and nutritious meal.

- **Sustainability:** Simple to prepare and versatile, the stew can be modified with different beans or vegetables to keep it varied and exciting.

NUTRITIONAL VALUES:

Calories: 270 kcal | Protein: 1.0 oz | Carbohydrates: 1.5 oz | Fiber: 0.8 oz | Fat: 0.6 oz

TOFU STIR-FRY WITH MIXED VEGETABLES

PREPARATION TIME: 10 min.

COOKING TIME: 20 min.

SERVINGS: 2 servings

TARGETED INGREDIENTS:

- 6 oz firm tofu, cubed (high in plant-based protein)
- 1 cup broccoli florets (fiber, low in calories)
- 1/2 cup sliced bell peppers (rich in vitamins, low in calories)
- 1/2 cup sliced carrots (adds sweetness, high in fiber)
- 1 Tbsp low-sodium soy sauce (flavor without excess sodium)
- 1 tsp olive oil (healthy fats)
- 1 clove garlic, minced (flavor without calories)
- Salt and pepper to taste (use sparingly to control sodium intake)

INSTRUCTIONS FOCUSED ON DR. NOWZARADAN'S PLAN:

1. **Cook the Tofu:** In a non-stick pan, heat 1 tsp olive oil over medium heat. Add the cubed tofu and cook for 5-7 minutes, turning occasionally, until golden brown.

2. **Add the Vegetables:** Add 1 cup broccoli, 1/2 cup bell peppers, and 1/2 cup carrots to the pan. Stir in 1 minced garlic clove and cook for 5 minutes until the vegetables are tender.

3. **Season and Serve:** Stir in 1 Tbsp soy sauce and cook for another 2 minutes. Serve the stir-fry hot for a filling, plant-based dinner.

TIPS FOR QUICK AND SUSTAINABLE PREPARATION:

- **Make-Ahead:** Prepare the tofu ahead of time and store it in the refrigerator for quick meals.

- **Batch Cooking:** Double the recipe and store leftovers for easy lunches or dinners.

ADAPTATIONS FOR LONG-TERM SUCCESS:

- **Balanced Nutrition:** This stir-fry is rich in plant-based protein and vegetables, making it a balanced and satisfying meal.

- **Sustainability:** The recipe is highly versatile, allowing you to swap in different vegetables or proteins like tempeh for variety.

NUTRITIONAL VALUES:

Calories: 300 kcal | Protein: 1.4 oz | Carbohydrates: 1.0 oz | Fiber: 0.5 oz | Fat: 0.8 oz

QUINOA AND ROASTED VEGETABLE BOWL

PREPARATION TIME: 15 min.

COOKING TIME: 30 min.

SERVINGS: 2 servings

TARGETED INGREDIENTS:

- 1/2 cup cooked quinoa (complete protein, rich in fiber)
- 1/2 cup broccoli florets (fiber, low in calories)
- 1/2 cup diced sweet potatoes (adds sweetness, high in fiber)
- 1/2 cup sliced bell peppers (rich in vitamins, low in calories)
- 1 tsp olive oil (healthy fats)
- 1 tsp balsamic vinegar (optional, for flavor)
- Salt and pepper to taste (use sparingly to control sodium intake)

INSTRUCTIONS FOCUSED ON DR. NOWZARADAN'S PLAN:

1. **Prepare the Vegetables:** Preheat the oven to 375°F (190°C). Arrange 1/2 cup diced sweet potatoes, 1/2 cup broccoli, and 1/2 cup bell peppers on a baking sheet. Drizzle with 1 tsp olive oil and season with salt and pepper.

2. **Roast the Vegetables:** Roast in the preheated oven for 25-30 minutes, until the vegetables are tender and slightly caramelized.

3. **Assemble the Bowl:** In a serving bowl, layer the cooked quinoa with the roasted vegetables. Drizzle with 1 tsp balsamic vinegar if desired.

4. **Serve:** Enjoy immediately as a hearty, plant-based dinner.

TIPS FOR QUICK AND SUSTAINABLE PREPARATION:

- **Advance Prep:** Cook the quinoa and roast the vegetables ahead of time for easy assembly later.
- **Batch Cooking:** Prepare extra vegetables and quinoa for ready-made meals during the week.

ADAPTATIONS FOR LONG-TERM SUCCESS:

- **Balanced Nutrition:** This bowl offers a combination of plant-based protein, fiber, and essential nutrients, ensuring a satisfying and well-rounded meal.
- **Sustainability:** The recipe is flexible, allowing for different vegetables or grains to keep it varied and enjoyable.

NUTRITIONAL VALUES:

Calories: 320 kcal | Protein: 1.2 oz | Carbohydrates: 1.6 oz | Fiber: 0.7 oz | Fat: 0.8 oz

CHICKPEA AND SPINACH CURRY

PREPARATION TIME: 10 min.

COOKING TIME: 25 min.

SERVINGS: 2 servings

TARGETED INGREDIENTS:

- 1 cup cooked chickpeas (plant-based protein, high in fiber)
- 2 cups fresh spinach (low in calories, rich in iron and vitamins)
- 1/2 cup diced tomatoes (adds flavor, low in calories)
- 1/4 cup diced onion (flavor, low in calories)
- 1 clove garlic, minced (flavor without calories)
- 1 tsp curry powder (optional, for flavor)
- 1 tsp olive oil (healthy fats)
- Salt and pepper to taste (use sparingly to control sodium intake)

INSTRUCTIONS FOCUSED ON DR. NOWZARADAN'S PLAN:

1. **Cook the Aromatics:** In a large pot, heat 1 tsp olive oil over medium heat. Add 1/4 cup diced onion and 1 minced garlic clove, cooking until translucent.

2. **Add the Chickpeas and Tomatoes:** Stir in 1 cup cooked chickpeas, 1/2 cup diced tomatoes, and 1 tsp curry powder. Cook for 10 minutes, allowing the flavors to meld.

3. **Add the Spinach:** Stir in 2 cups fresh spinach and cook until wilted, about 2-3 minutes.

4. **Serve:** Ladle the curry into bowls and enjoy as a hearty, plant-based dinner.

TIPS FOR QUICK AND SUSTAINABLE PREPARATION:

- **Batch Cooking:** Make a large batch of curry and freeze individual portions for quick, ready-to-eat meals.
- **Advance Prep:** Chop the vegetables and cook the chickpeas ahead of time for quicker assembly.

ADAPTATIONS FOR LONG-TERM SUCCESS:

- **Balanced Nutrition:** This curry offers a combination of plant-based protein, fiber, and essential nutrients, making it a well-rounded meal.
- **Sustainability:** Simple to prepare and versatile, the curry can be modified with different beans or greens to keep it varied and exciting.

NUTRITIONAL VALUES:

Calories: 280 kcal | Protein: 1.0 oz | Carbohydrates: 1.5 oz | Fiber: 0.8 oz | Fat: 0.6 oz

SWEET POTATO AND BLACK BEAN TACOS

PREPARATION TIME: 15 min.
COOKING TIME: 20 min.
SERVINGS: 2 servings
TARGETED INGREDIENTS:

- 1 medium sweet potato, diced (adds sweetness, high in fiber)
- 1/2 cup black beans (plant-based protein, high in fiber)
- 1/4 cup diced tomatoes (adds flavor, low in calories)
- 1/4 cup diced onion (flavor, low in calories)
- 1 tsp cumin (optional, for flavor)
- 1 tsp olive oil (healthy fats)
- 4 small corn tortillas (low-calorie, high in fiber)
- Salt and pepper to taste (use sparingly to control sodium intake)

INSTRUCTIONS FOCUSED ON DR. NOWZARADAN'S PLAN:

1. **Roast the Sweet Potatoes:** Preheat the oven to 375°F (190°C). Arrange the diced sweet potatoes on a baking sheet, drizzle with 1 tsp olive oil, and season with salt, pepper, and cumin. Roast for 20 minutes until tender.
2. **Prepare the Tacos:** Warm the corn tortillas in a non-stick pan or directly on the stove over low heat. Once warm, fill each tortilla with roasted sweet potatoes, black beans, diced tomatoes, and diced onions.
3. **Serve:** Enjoy the tacos immediately as a filling, plant-based dinner.

TIPS FOR QUICK AND SUSTAINABLE PREPARATION:

- **Make-Ahead:** Roast the sweet potatoes ahead of time and store them in the refrigerator for quick meal assembly.
- **Batch Cooking:** Double the recipe and store leftovers for easy lunches or dinners.

ADAPTATIONS FOR LONG-TERM SUCCESS:

- **Balanced Nutrition:** These tacos offer a satisfying combination of plant-based protein, fiber, and essential nutrients, ensuring a well-rounded and enjoyable meal.
- **Sustainability:** The recipe is highly adaptable, allowing you to use different beans or vegetables to keep the tacos varied and exciting.

NUTRITIONAL VALUES:

Calories: 300 kcal | Protein: 1.0 oz | Carbohydrates: 1.6 oz | Fiber: 0.7 oz | Fat: 0.6 oz

CHAPTER 10: SNACK AND DESSERT RECIPES TO KEEP YOU ON TRACK

10.1 HEALTHY SNACKS FOR BETWEEN MEALS

APPLE SLICES WITH PEANUT BUTTER

PREPARATION TIME: 5 min.

SERVINGS: 2 servings

TARGETED INGREDIENTS:

- 1 medium apple, sliced (fiber, natural sweetness)
- 1 Tbsp natural peanut butter (healthy fats, protein)

INSTRUCTIONS FOCUSED ON DR. NOWZARADAN'S PLAN:

1. **Slice the Apple:** Core and slice 1 medium apple into wedges.
2. **Add Peanut Butter:** Spread a thin layer of peanut butter on each apple slice.

TIPS FOR QUICK AND SUSTAINABLE PREPARATION:

- **Make-Ahead:** Pre-slice the apple and store it in an airtight container with a splash of lemon juice to prevent browning.

- **Batch Prep:** Double the serving size for a more substantial snack if needed.

ADAPTATIONS FOR LONG-TERM SUCCESS:

- **Balanced Nutrition:** The combination of fiber from the apple and protein from the peanut butter makes this snack both filling and nutritious.
- **Sustainability:** This easy-to-prepare snack can be a staple in your diet, providing consistent energy without added sugars.

NUTRITIONAL VALUES:

Calories: 180 kcal | Protein: 0.5 oz | Carbohydrates: 1.0 oz | Fiber: 0.4 oz | Fat: 0.5 oz

ALMOND AND GREEK YOGURT PARFAIT

PREPARATION TIME: 5 min.

SERVINGS: 2 servings

TARGETED INGREDIENTS:

- 1/2 cup plain Greek yogurt (high in protein, low in fat)
- 1 Tbsp sliced almonds (healthy fats, adds crunch)
- 1/4 cup mixed berries (low in calories, high in fiber)
- 1 tsp honey (optional, for sweetness)

INSTRUCTIONS FOCUSED ON DR. NOWZARADAN'S PLAN:

1. **Prepare the Parfait:** In a small bowl, layer 1/4 cup of Greek yogurt at the bottom.
2. **Add the Berries:** Sprinkle 1/8 cup of mixed berries on top of the yogurt.
3. **Repeat Layers:** Add another layer of yogurt and berries.
4. **Top with Almonds:** Finish with 1 Tbsp sliced almonds for crunch.

5. **Optional Sweetness:** Drizzle 1 tsp of honey if desired.

TIPS FOR QUICK AND SUSTAINABLE PREPARATION:

- **Make-Ahead:** Assemble the parfait in a portable container the night before for an easy grab-and-go snack.
- **Variations:** Swap almonds for walnuts or add chia seeds for an extra fiber boost.

ADAPTATIONS FOR LONG-TERM SUCCESS:

- **Balanced Nutrition:** This parfait offers a perfect mix of protein, healthy fats, and fiber, keeping you full and satisfied.
- **Sustainability:** The simple ingredients make this snack easy to keep on hand and adapt to your preferences.

NUTRITIONAL VALUES:

Calories: 160 kcal | Protein: 0.7 oz | Carbohydrates: 0.5 oz | Fiber: 0.2 oz | Fat: 0.4 oz

CUCUMBER AND HUMMUS BITES

PREPARATION TIME: 5 min.

SERVINGS: 2 servings

TARGETED INGREDIENTS:

- 1/2 cucumber, sliced (low in calories, hydrating)
- 1/4 cup hummus (plant-based protein, high in fiber)
- 1 tsp sesame seeds (optional, for texture)

INSTRUCTIONS FOCUSED ON DR. NOWZARADAN'S PLAN:

1. **Prepare the Cucumber:** Slice 1/2 cucumber into rounds, about 1/4 inch thick.
2. **Add the Hummus:** Spread 1/2 tsp of hummus onto each cucumber slice.
3. **Optional Garnish:** Sprinkle with sesame seeds for added texture.

TIPS FOR QUICK AND SUSTAINABLE PREPARATION:

- **Make-Ahead:** Prepare the cucumber slices in advance and store them in the refrigerator for easy assembly.
- **Batch Prep:** Double the ingredients to make enough for multiple snacks throughout the day.

ADAPTATIONS FOR LONG-TERM SUCCESS:

- **Balanced Nutrition:** This snack combines hydrating cucumber with protein-rich hummus for a refreshing and satisfying bite.
- **Sustainability:** The ingredients are simple and versatile, making it easy to incorporate into your daily routine.

NUTRITIONAL VALUES:

Calories: 100 kcal | Protein: 0.4 oz | Carbohydrates: 0.5 oz | Fiber: 0.2 oz | Fat: 0.3 oz

HARD-BOILED EGGS WITH AVOCADO

PREPARATION TIME: 5 min.

COOKING TIME: 10 min.

SERVINGS: 2 servings

TARGETED INGREDIENTS:

- 2 hard-boiled eggs (high in protein, low in carbs)
- 1/4 avocado, sliced (healthy fats, fiber)
- Salt and pepper to taste (use sparingly to control sodium intake)

INSTRUCTIONS FOCUSED ON DR. NOWZARADAN'S PLAN:

1. **Boil the Eggs:** Place eggs in a pot of cold water, bring to a boil, and cook for 10 minutes. Cool under cold running water and peel.
2. **Slice and Serve:** Slice the eggs and avocado, season with salt and pepper, and enjoy.

TIPS FOR QUICK AND SUSTAINABLE PREPARATION:

- **Make-Ahead:** Boil a batch of eggs at the beginning of the week for quick snacks.
- **Batch Prep:** Prepare extra avocado slices and store them with the pit to prevent browning.

ADAPTATIONS FOR LONG-TERM SUCCESS:

- **Balanced Nutrition:** This snack offers a combination of protein and healthy fats, ensuring a filling and nutritious option.
- **Sustainability:** Easy to prepare and versatile, this snack can be a go-to for those on Dr. Nowzaradan's plan.

NUTRITIONAL VALUES:

Calories: 220 kcal | Protein: 0.8 oz | Carbohydrates: 0.2 oz | Fiber: 0.3 oz | Fat: 1.4 oz

MIXED NUTS AND DRIED FRUIT

PREPARATION TIME: 2 min.

TARGETED INGREDIENTS:

SERVINGS: 2 servings

- 1/4 cup mixed nuts (healthy fats, protein)
- 2 Tbsp dried fruit (natural sweetness, fiber)

INSTRUCTIONS FOCUSED ON DR. NOWZARADAN'S PLAN:

1. **Measure the Ingredients:** Combine 1/4 cup mixed nuts with 2 Tbsp dried fruit in a small bowl.

TIPS FOR QUICK AND SUSTAINABLE PREPARATION:

- **Portion Control:** Pre-portion into small containers to avoid overeating.
- **Batch Prep:** Prepare multiple servings in advance for easy access throughout the week.

ADAPTATIONS FOR LONG-TERM SUCCESS:

- **Balanced Nutrition:** This snack offers a balance of protein, fiber, and healthy fats, making it both satisfying and nutritious.

- **Sustainability:** The ingredients are shelf-stable and portable, making this an ideal snack for busy lifestyles.

NUTRITIONAL VALUES:

Calories: 200 kcal | Protein: 0.4 oz | Carbohydrates: 0.9 oz | Fiber: 0.4 oz | Fat: 1.3 oz

CARROT STICKS WITH GREEK YOGURT DIP

PREPARATION TIME: 5 min.

SERVINGS: 2 servings

TARGETED INGREDIENTS:

- 1 cup carrot sticks (low in calories, high in fiber)
- 1/4 cup plain Greek yogurt (high in protein, low in fat)
- 1 tsp lemon juice (adds flavor)
- 1/2 tsp dried dill (optional, for flavor)
- Salt and pepper to taste (use sparingly to control sodium intake)

INSTRUCTIONS FOCUSED ON DR. NOWZARADAN'S PLAN:

1. **Prepare the Carrots:** Wash and cut the carrots into sticks.
2. **Make the Dip:** In a small bowl, mix 1/4 cup Greek yogurt with 1 tsp lemon juice, 1/2 tsp dried dill, and a pinch of salt and pepper.
3. **Serve:** Dip the carrot sticks into the yogurt and enjoy.

TIPS FOR QUICK AND SUSTAINABLE PREPARATION:

- **Make-Ahead:** Pre-cut the carrot sticks and store them in water in the fridge for easy snacking.
- **Batch Prep:** Make extra dip and store it in the refrigerator for multiple snacks.

ADAPTATIONS FOR LONG-TERM SUCCESS:

- **Balanced Nutrition:** This snack combines fiber-rich carrots with protein-packed yogurt, ensuring a filling and healthy option.

- **Sustainability:** The simple ingredients make this snack easy to incorporate into a daily routine.

NUTRITIONAL VALUES:

Calories: 120 kcal | Protein: 0.6 oz | Carbohydrates: 0.7 oz | Fiber: 0.3 oz | Fat: 0.2 oz

COTTAGE CHEESE WITH PINEAPPLE

PREPARATION TIME: 3 min.

SERVINGS: 2

TARGETED INGREDIENTS:

- 1/2 cup low-fat cottage cheese (high in protein, low in fat)
- 1/4 cup pineapple chunks (natural sweetness, fiber)

INSTRUCTIONS FOCUSED ON DR. NOWZARADAN'S PLAN:

1. **Combine the Ingredients:** In a small bowl, mix 1/2 cup cottage cheese with 1/4 cup pineapple chunks.
2. **Serve:** Enjoy as a quick and refreshing snack.

TIPS FOR QUICK AND SUSTAINABLE PREPARATION:

- **Make-Ahead:** Pre-portion the cottage cheese and pineapple into small containers for easy grab-and-go snacks.
- **Batch Prep:** Prepare enough for a few days and store in the refrigerator.

ADAPTATIONS FOR LONG-TERM SUCCESS:

- **Balanced Nutrition:** This snack offers a balance of protein and natural sugars, keeping you full and satisfied between meals.
- **Sustainability:** The simplicity of this snack makes it easy to prepare and enjoy regularly.

NUTRITIONAL VALUES:

Calories: 150 kcal | Protein: 0.7 oz | Carbohydrates: 0.8 oz | Fiber: 0.2 oz | Fat: 0.3 oz

10.2 GUILT-FREE DESSERTS

CHOCOLATE AVOCADO MOUSSE

PREPARATION TIME: 10 min.

SERVINGS: 2

TARGETED INGREDIENTS:

- 1 ripe avocado (healthy fats, creamy texture)
- 2 Tbsp unsweetened cocoa powder (rich in antioxidants, low in sugar)
- 1-2 Tbsp maple syrup or honey (natural sweetness, use sparingly)
- 1 tsp vanilla extract (adds flavor)
- A pinch of salt (enhances the chocolate flavor)

INSTRUCTIONS FOCUSED ON DR. NOWZARADAN'S PLAN:

1. **Blend Ingredients:** In a food processor, combine the avocado, cocoa powder, maple syrup, vanilla extract, and salt.
2. **Process:** Blend until smooth and creamy, scraping down the sides as needed.
3. **Serve:** Divide the mousse into small bowls or ramekins and refrigerate for at least 30 minutes before serving.

TIPS FOR QUICK AND SUSTAINABLE PREPARATION:

- **Advance Prep:** Make this dessert the night before for a ready-to-eat treat.
- **Batch Prep:** Double the recipe and store servings in the refrigerator for a few days.

ADAPTATIONS FOR LONG-TERM SUCCESS:

- **Balanced Nutrition:** This mousse provides healthy fats and antioxidants, making it a satisfying yet nutritious dessert.
- **Sustainability:** Easy to prepare and store, this dessert can become a regular part of your diet without derailing your progress.

NUTRITIONAL VALUES:

Calories: 180 kcal | Protein: 0.5 oz | Fat: 1 oz | Carbohydrates: 0.6 oz | Fiber: 0.3 oz

BERRY YOGURT PARFAIT

PREPARATION TIME: 5 min.

SERVINGS: 2

TARGETED INGREDIENTS:

- 1/2 cup plain Greek yogurt (high in protein, low in sugar)
- 1/4 cup mixed berries (antioxidants, natural sweetness)
- 1 Tbsp honey or agave syrup (optional, for extra sweetness)
- 1 Tbsp granola (for crunch, use sparingly)

INSTRUCTIONS FOCUSED ON DR. NOWZARADAN'S PLAN:

1. **Layer Ingredients:** In a glass or bowl, layer half of the yogurt, then half of the berries. Repeat with remaining yogurt and berries.
2. **Top with Granola:** Sprinkle the granola on top for added texture.
3. **Optional Sweetness:** Drizzle with honey or agave if desired.

TIPS FOR QUICK AND SUSTAINABLE PREPARATION:

- **Make-Ahead:** Assemble parfaits in small jars for a ready-to-go snack or dessert.
- **Batch Prep:** Prepare multiple servings and store in the refrigerator for up to 3 days.

ADAPTATIONS FOR LONG-TERM SUCCESS:

- **Balanced Nutrition:** Offers a mix of protein, fiber, and healthy carbs to keep you full and satisfied.
- **Sustainability:** A quick and easy dessert that can be customized with different fruits and toppings.

NUTRITIONAL VALUES:

Calories: 150 kcal | Protein: 0.7 oz | Fat: 0.2 oz | Carbohydrates: 0.8 oz | Fiber: 0.2 oz

BAKED CINNAMON APPLES

PREPARATION TIME: 5 min.

COOKING TIME: 20 min.

SERVINGS: 2

TARGETED INGREDIENTS:

- 2 medium apples (fiber-rich, natural sweetness)
- 1 tsp cinnamon (spices, metabolism boost)
- 1 Tbsp maple syrup (natural sweetness)
- 1 Tbsp chopped nuts (optional, adds crunch and healthy fats)

INSTRUCTIONS FOCUSED ON DR. NOWZARADAN'S PLAN:

1. **Preheat Oven:** Preheat oven to 350°F (175°C).
2. **Prepare Apples:** Core and slice the apples, placing them in a baking dish.
3. **Add Flavor:** Sprinkle with cinnamon and drizzle with maple syrup.
4. **Bake:** Bake for 20 minutes or until the apples are tender.
5. **Optional Nuts:** Sprinkle chopped nuts over the top before serving.

TIPS FOR QUICK AND SUSTAINABLE PREPARATION:

- **Batch Cooking:** Make a large batch and store in the refrigerator for easy reheating.
- **Quick Prep:** Use an apple corer to speed up preparation.

ADAPTATIONS FOR LONG-TERM SUCCESS:

- **Balanced Nutrition:** Provides natural sweetness and fiber, making it a satisfying and nutritious dessert.
- **Sustainability:** Simple ingredients and quick preparation make this a regular dessert option.

NUTRITIONAL VALUES:

Calories: 130 kcal | Protein: 0.2 oz | Fat: 0.1 oz | Carbohydrates: 0.8 oz | Fiber: 0.4 oz

BANANA ICE CREAM

PREPARATION TIME: 5 min.

COOKING TIME: 0 min. (Freeze for 2 hours)

SERVINGS: 2

TARGETED INGREDIENTS:

- 2 ripe bananas (natural sweetness, creamy texture)

INSTRUCTIONS FOCUSED ON DR. NOWZARADAN'S PLAN:

1. **Freeze Bananas:** Peel and slice the bananas, then freeze for at least 2 hours.
2. **Blend:** Place frozen banana slices in a food processor and blend until smooth and creamy.
3. **Serve:** Scoop into bowls and enjoy immediately.

TIPS FOR QUICK AND SUSTAINABLE PREPARATION:

- **Advance Prep:** Keep a stash of frozen banana slices in the freezer for instant ice cream.
- **Flavor Variations:** Add a teaspoon of cocoa powder or vanilla extract for different flavors.

ADAPTATIONS FOR LONG-TERM SUCCESS:

- **Balanced Nutrition:** This dessert is low in calories but high in fiber and potassium, making it a guilt-free treat.
- **Sustainability:** It's easy to prepare and can be enjoyed regularly as a healthy dessert option.

NUTRITIONAL VALUES:

Calories: 105 kcal | Protein: 0.3 oz | Fat: 0.1 oz | Carbohydrates: 1.1 oz | Fiber: 0.3 oz

CHIA SEED PUDDING

PREPARATION TIME: 5 min.

COOKING TIME: 0 min. (Chill for 2 hours)

SERVINGS: 2

TARGETED INGREDIENTS:

- 3 Tbsp chia seeds (rich in fiber, omega-3s)
- 1 cup unsweetened almond milk (low in calories, dairy-free)
- 1 tsp vanilla extract (adds flavor)
- 1 Tbsp honey or maple syrup (optional, natural sweetness)

INSTRUCTIONS FOCUSED ON DR. NOWZARADAN'S PLAN:

1. **Mix Ingredients:** In a bowl, whisk together the chia seeds, almond milk, vanilla extract, and sweetener if using.
2. **Chill:** Refrigerate for at least 2 hours, or until the chia seeds have absorbed the liquid and the mixture has thickened.
3. **Serve:** Stir the pudding and top with fresh fruit if desired.

TIPS FOR QUICK AND SUSTAINABLE PREPARATION:

- **Make-Ahead:** Prepare a batch and store in the refrigerator for easy snacking throughout the week.
- **Flavor Variations:** Add cocoa powder or cinnamon for different flavors.

ADAPTATIONS FOR LONG-TERM SUCCESS:

- **Balanced Nutrition:** High in fiber and healthy fats, this pudding is a nutritious dessert that keeps you full.
- **Sustainability:** Easy to prepare and customize, making it a versatile option for any diet.

NUTRITIONAL VALUES:

Calories: 150 kcal | Protein: 0.3 oz | Fat: 0.8 oz | Carbohydrates: 0.4 oz | Fiber: 0.4 oz

CHOCOLATE-DIPPED STRAWBERRIES

PREPARATION TIME: 5 min.

COOKING TIME: 5 min.

SERVINGS: 2

TARGETED INGREDIENTS:

- 10 fresh strawberries (low in calories, rich in vitamins)
- 2 oz dark chocolate (antioxidants, rich flavor)

INSTRUCTIONS FOCUSED ON DR. NOWZARADAN'S PLAN:

1. **Melt Chocolate:** In a microwave-safe bowl, melt the dark chocolate in 20-second intervals, stirring between each, until smooth.
2. **Dip Strawberries:** Dip each strawberry into the melted chocolate, covering about two-thirds of the berry.
3. **Chill:** Place the dipped strawberries on a parchment-lined tray and refrigerate for about 10 minutes to set the chocolate.

TIPS FOR QUICK AND SUSTAINABLE PREPARATION:

- **Make-Ahead:** Prepare these the night before for a quick, ready-to-eat treat.
- **Batch Prep:** Double the recipe for a small gathering or to enjoy over several days.

ADAPTATIONS FOR LONG-TERM SUCCESS:

- **Balanced Nutrition:** Combines the antioxidants of dark chocolate with the vitamins and fiber of strawberries.
- **Sustainability:** Easy to make and store, making it a regular dessert option.

NUTRITIONAL VALUES:

Calories: 120 kcal | Protein: 0.4 oz | Fat: 0.8 oz | Carbohydrates: 0.4 oz | Fiber: 0.3 oz

ALMOND BUTTER COOKIES

PREPARATION TIME: 5 min.

COOKING TIME: 10 min.

SERVINGS: 2

TARGETED INGREDIENTS:

- 1 cup almond butter (healthy fats, protein)
- 1/4 cup honey or maple syrup (natural sweetness)
- 1 egg (protein, helps bind ingredients)
- 1/2 tsp baking soda (for texture)
- 1 tsp vanilla extract (adds flavor)

INSTRUCTIONS FOCUSED ON DR. NOWZARADAN'S PLAN:

1. **Preheat Oven:** Preheat oven to 350°F (175°C).
2. **Mix Ingredients:** In a bowl, combine almond butter, honey, egg, baking soda, and vanilla extract. Mix until smooth.
3. **Shape Cookies:** Drop tablespoon-sized balls of dough onto a parchment-lined baking sheet, flattening slightly with a fork.
4. **Bake:** Bake for 10 minutes, or until the edges are golden brown.
5. **Cool:** Allow cookies to cool on the baking sheet for 5 minutes before transferring to a wire rack.

TIPS FOR QUICK AND SUSTAINABLE PREPARATION:

- **Batch Prep:** Make a double batch and freeze half for later.
- **Quick Prep:** No need for flour, making this a fast and simple recipe.

ADAPTATIONS FOR LONG-TERM SUCCESS:

- **Balanced Nutrition:** These cookies are low in carbs and sugar but provide healthy fats and protein, making them a smart dessert choice.
- **Sustainability:** Simple ingredients and quick preparation make these cookies a convenient treat that aligns with a healthy lifestyle.

NUTRITIONAL VALUES:

Calories: 180 kcal | Protein: 0.7 oz | Fat: 1 oz | Carbohydrates: 0.3 oz | Fiber: 0.2 oz

10.3 SMART INDULGENCES

DARK CHOCOLATE ALMOND CLUSTERS

PREPARATION TIME: 10 min.

COOKING TIME: 0 min.

SERVINGS: 2

TARGETED INGREDIENTS:

- 1/2 cup raw almonds (healthy fats, protein, and fiber)
- 2 oz dark chocolate (antioxidants, low in sugar)

INSTRUCTIONS FOCUSED ON DR. NOWZARADAN'S PLAN:

1. **Melt the Chocolate:** In a microwave-safe bowl, melt the dark chocolate in 20-second intervals, stirring between each, until smooth.
2. **Coat the Almonds:** Mix the almonds into the melted chocolate until they are fully coated.
3. **Form Clusters:** Drop spoonsful of the chocolate-almond mixture onto a parchment-lined baking sheet.
4. **Chill:** Place the baking sheet in the refrigerator for about 20 minutes until the clusters are firm.

TIPS FOR QUICK AND SUSTAINABLE PREPARATION:

- **Make-Ahead:** Prepare a batch and store in an airtight container in the refrigerator.
- **Portion Control:** Limit yourself to one or two clusters per serving to keep calories in check.

ADAPTATIONS FOR LONG-TERM SUCCESS:

- **Balanced Nutrition:** Provides a combination of healthy fats, protein, and fiber, making it a satisfying treat.

- **Sustainability:** Easy to prepare and store, ensuring you can enjoy a treat without compromising your diet.

NUTRITIONAL VALUES:

Calories: 180 kcal | Protein: 0.8 oz | Fat: 1.1 oz | Carbohydrates: 0.4 oz | Fiber: 0.3 oz

PEANUT BUTTER APPLE SLICES

PREPARATION TIME: 5 min.

COOKING TIME: 0 min.

SERVINGS: 2

TARGETED INGREDIENTS:

- 1 medium apple (fiber-rich, natural sweetness)
- 2 Tbsp natural peanut butter (healthy fats, protein)

INSTRUCTIONS FOCUSED ON DR. NOWZARADAN'S PLAN:

1. **Slice the Apple:** Cut the apple into thin slices.
2. **Add Peanut Butter:** Spread a thin layer of peanut butter on each apple slice.
3. **Serve:** Arrange the slices on a plate and enjoy.

TIPS FOR QUICK AND SUSTAINABLE PREPARATION:

- **On-the-Go:** Pack apple slices and a small container of peanut butter for a portable snack.
- **Batch Prep:** Pre-slice apples and store in an airtight container to save time.

ADAPTATIONS FOR LONG-TERM SUCCESS:

- **Balanced Nutrition:** Combines fiber, healthy fats, and protein to keep you full and energized.
- **Sustainability:** Simple and quick, making it a regular part of your snack routine.

NUTRITIONAL VALUES:

Calories: 190 kcal | Protein: 0.7 oz | Fat: 0.9 oz | Carbohydrates: 1.2 oz | Fiber: 0.4 oz

FROZEN YOGURT BITES

PREPARATION TIME: 10 min.

COOKING TIME: 0 min. (Freeze for 2 hours)

SERVINGS: 2

TARGETED INGREDIENTS:

- 1/2 cup plain Greek yogurt (high in protein, low in sugar)
- 1/4 cup mixed berries (antioxidants, natural sweetness)
- 1 tsp honey (optional, for added sweetness)

INSTRUCTIONS FOCUSED ON DR. NOWZARADAN'S PLAN:

1. **Mix Ingredients:** In a bowl, combine the Greek yogurt, mixed berries, and honey.
2. **Portion into Molds:** Spoon the mixture into silicone molds or small muffin liners.
3. **Freeze:** Place in the freezer for at least 2 hours or until solid.
4. **Serve:** Pop the frozen bites out of the molds and enjoy immediately.

TIPS FOR QUICK AND SUSTAINABLE PREPARATION:

- **Batch Prep:** Make a large batch and store in the freezer for a ready-to-eat treat.
- **Portion Control:** Pre-portion the bites to avoid overeating.

ADAPTATIONS FOR LONG-TERM SUCCESS:

- **Balanced Nutrition:** Offers a combination of protein and antioxidants, making it a nutritious dessert or snack.
- **Sustainability:** Easy to prepare and store, ensuring you always have a healthy treat on hand.

NUTRITIONAL VALUES:

Calories: 80 kcal | Protein: 0.6 oz | Fat: 0.2 oz | Carbohydrates: 0.5 oz | Fiber: 0.1 oz

DARK CHOCOLATE AND BANANA SLICES

PREPARATION TIME: 5 min.

COOKING TIME: 0 min.

SERVINGS: 2

TARGETED INGREDIENTS:

- 1 medium banana (fiber, natural sweetness)
- 1 oz dark chocolate (antioxidants, low in sugar)

INSTRUCTIONS FOCUSED ON DR. NOWZARADAN'S PLAN:

1. **Melt the Chocolate:** In a microwave-safe bowl, melt the dark chocolate in 20-second intervals, stirring between each, until smooth.
2. **Slice the Banana:** Cut the banana into 1/2-inch slices.
3. **Dip in Chocolate:** Dip each banana slice halfway into the melted chocolate.
4. **Chill:** Place the slices on a parchment-lined plate and refrigerate for 10 minutes or until the chocolate is set.

TIPS FOR QUICK AND SUSTAINABLE PREPARATION:

- **Batch Prep:** Prepare multiple servings and store in the refrigerator for a quick treat.
- **Portion Control:** Limit yourself to a small number of slices to manage calorie intake.

ADAPTATIONS FOR LONG-TERM SUCCESS:

- **Balanced Nutrition:** Combines the fiber and potassium of bananas with the antioxidants of dark chocolate, creating a nutritious snack.
- **Sustainability:** Quick and easy to make, ensuring you can enjoy a treat without guilt.

NUTRITIONAL VALUES:

Calories: 120 kcal | Protein: 0.4 oz | Fat: 0.4 oz | Carbohydrates: 0.9 oz | Fiber: 0.3 oz

MINI RICE CAKE SANDWICHES

PREPARATION TIME: 5 min.
COOKING TIME: 0 min.
SERVINGS: 2
TARGETED INGREDIENTS:

- 4 mini rice cakes (light and crunchy, low in calories)
- 2 Tbsp almond butter (healthy fats, protein)
- 1 Tbsp unsweetened shredded coconut (adds texture and flavor)

INSTRUCTIONS FOCUSED ON DR. NOWZARADAN'S PLAN:

1. **Spread Almond Butter:** Spread a thin layer of almond butter on two of the rice cakes.
2. **Add Coconut:** Sprinkle unsweetened shredded coconut over the almond butter.
3. **Assemble:** Top with the remaining rice cakes to create mini sandwiches.

TIPS FOR QUICK AND SUSTAINABLE PREPARATION:

- **Batch Prep:** Prepare several mini sandwiches and store in an airtight container.
- **On-the-Go:** Pack these sandwiches for a portable snack.

ADAPTATIONS FOR LONG-TERM SUCCESS:

- **Balanced Nutrition:** Combines the crunch of rice cakes with the protein and healthy fats of almond butter.
- **Sustainability:** Easy to prepare and store, making it a convenient snack option.

NUTRITIONAL VALUES:

- **Balanced Nutrition:** Provides natural sweetness with fiber and healthy fats, making it a satisfying and nutritious dessert.
- **Sustainability:** Simple ingredients and easy preparation make this a regular dessert option.

NUTRITIONAL VALUES:
Calories: 150 kcal | Protein: 0.2 oz | Fat: 0.3 oz | Carbohydrates: 1.0 oz | Fiber: 0.5 oz

Calories: 130 kcal | Protein: 0.4 oz | Fat: 0.8 oz | Carbohydrates: 0.7 oz | Fiber: 0.2 oz

CINNAMON BAKED PEARS

PREPARATION TIME: 5 min.
COOKING TIME: 20 min.
SERVINGS: 2
TARGETED INGREDIENTS:

- 2 medium pears (fiber-rich, natural sweetness)
- 1 tsp cinnamon (adds warmth, boosts metabolism)
- 1 Tbsp chopped walnuts (optional, adds healthy fats and crunch)

INSTRUCTIONS FOCUSED ON DR. NOWZARADAN'S PLAN:

1. **Preheat Oven:** Preheat oven to 350°F (175°C).
2. **Prepare Pears:** Halve the pears and remove the cores. Place them in a baking dish.
3. **Add Flavor:** Sprinkle with cinnamon and top with chopped walnuts if using.
4. **Bake:** Bake for 20 minutes or until tender.
5. **Serve:** Serve warm, optionally with a dollop of Greek yogurt.

TIPS FOR QUICK AND SUSTAINABLE PREPARATION:

- **Batch Prep:** Bake multiple pears and store in the refrigerator for a ready-to-eat dessert.
- **Quick Option:** Microwave the pears for 3-4 minutes instead of baking for a faster preparation.

ADAPTATIONS FOR LONG-TERM SUCCESS:

COCONUT CHIA PUDDING

PREPARATION TIME: 5 min.
COOKING TIME: 0 min. (Chill for 2 hours)
SERVINGS: 2
TARGETED INGREDIENTS:

- 3 Tbsp chia seeds (high in fiber and omega-3s)
- 1 cup unsweetened coconut milk (adds creaminess, low in calories)
- 1 tsp vanilla extract (adds flavor)

- 1 Tbsp unsweetened shredded coconut (optional, adds texture)

INSTRUCTIONS FOCUSED ON DR. NOWZARADAN'S PLAN:

1. **Mix Ingredients:** In a bowl, whisk together the chia seeds, coconut milk, vanilla extract, and shredded coconut.
2. **Chill:** Refrigerate for at least 2 hours, or until the mixture thickens.
3. **Serve:** Stir the pudding and top with additional shredded coconut if desired.

TIPS FOR QUICK AND SUSTAINABLE PREPARATION:

- **Make-Ahead:** Prepare a batch and store in the refrigerator for easy snacking throughout the week.
- **Flavor Variations:** Add cocoa powder or fresh fruit for different flavors.

ADAPTATIONS FOR LONG-TERM SUCCESS:

- **Balanced Nutrition:** High in fiber and healthy fats, this pudding is a nutritious dessert that keeps you full.
- **Sustainability:** Easy to prepare and customize, making it a versatile option for any diet.

NUTRITIONAL VALUES:

Calories: 160 kcal | Protein: 0.3 oz | Fat: 0.9 oz | Carbohydrates: 0.4 oz | Fiber: 0.5 oz

11.1 THE BASICS OF MEAL PREP

Meal prep, often hailed as the cornerstone of successful, sustainable eating, is more than just a time-saving strategy. It's a powerful tool that empowers you to take control of your diet, ensuring that healthy, nutritious meals are always within reach. At its core, meal prep is about planning ahead—envisioning your week, understanding your nutritional needs, and preparing for success. But while it may seem straightforward, mastering meal prep requires a blend of foresight, organization, and a little creativity.

The first step to effective meal prep is setting your intentions. Think about your goals: Are you looking to lose weight, build muscle, or simply maintain a balanced diet? Your objectives will shape the type of meals you prepare. For those following Dr. Nowzaradan's plan, the focus is on low-calorie, nutrient-dense foods that promote satiety without excess calories. Keeping this in mind will guide your choices as you plan and prepare your meals.

Once your goals are clear, the next step is to design a menu that aligns with them. This isn't just about picking recipes; it's about creating a plan that fits seamlessly into your life. Consider your schedule: How much time do you have to cook each day? Are there days when you'll need something quick and easy, or can you afford to spend a little more time in the kitchen? The key is to strike a balance between variety and simplicity—enough diversity to keep your meals interesting, but not so much that you're overwhelmed by the preparation.

With your menu in hand, it's time to shop. This is where organization really pays off. A well-thought-out shopping list, based on your planned meals, will save you time, reduce food waste, and help you stick to your nutritional goals. As you navigate the aisles, focus on whole foods—fresh vegetables, lean proteins, and healthy fats. These are the building blocks of a nutritious diet, and having them on hand will make meal prep easier and more efficient.

Now comes the heart of meal prep: the actual preparation. Set aside a few hours once or twice a week to cook and portion out your meals. This is where the magic happens, transforming raw ingredients into ready-to-eat meals that are convenient and aligned with your dietary goals. Whether you're grilling chicken breasts, roasting vegetables, or preparing overnight oats, the key is consistency. Stick to your plan, and don't be afraid to double recipes or batch-cook to save even more time.

As you portion out your meals, consider the importance of balance. Each meal should be a harmonious blend of protein, carbohydrates, and fats, tailored to your specific needs. Pay attention to portion sizes—too much or too little of any one component can derail your efforts. Investing in a good set of meal prep containers can make this process easier, helping you keep your portions in check and your meals fresh.

Finally, remember that meal prep is a skill, and like any skill, it takes practice. Your first few attempts might not be perfect, and that's okay. The key is to keep refining your approach, learning from what works and what doesn't, and adjusting your plan as needed. Over time, you'll find that meal prep not only saves you time and effort but also plays a crucial role in maintaining your health and well-being.

By mastering the basics of meal prep, you set yourself up for success, ensuring that healthy eating becomes a consistent and manageable part of your life.

11.2 BATCH COOKING FOR THE WEEK AHEAD

Batch cooking, a technique often praised by nutritionists and time-strapped individuals alike, is more than just a way to save time in the kitchen. It's a strategic approach to meal preparation that can help you stay on track with your dietary goals, reduce food waste, and ensure you always have healthy meals on hand. At its core, batch cooking involves preparing large quantities of food at once, which you can then portion out and enjoy throughout the week.

The beauty of batch cooking lies in its efficiency. Imagine coming home after a long day, tired and hungry, and knowing that a healthy, home-cooked meal is just minutes away. No need to reach for takeout menus or resort to unhealthy snacks; with batch cooking, your meals are ready and waiting. This approach not only saves time but also removes the stress of daily cooking, allowing you to focus on other aspects of your life while still maintaining a balanced diet.

To begin batch cooking, start by selecting recipes that lend themselves well to being made in large quantities. Think hearty soups, stews, casseroles, and roasted proteins like chicken breasts or tofu. These dishes can be cooked in bulk without compromising on flavor or nutritional value. Once you've chosen your recipes, make a comprehensive shopping list. Buying ingredients in bulk is often more economical, and with a well-planned list, you'll ensure you have everything you need to execute your meals efficiently.

When it comes to the actual cooking, organization is key. Set aside a dedicated time—perhaps a weekend afternoon—where you can focus solely on preparing your meals. Lay out all your ingredients, preheat the oven, and get your cooking stations ready. The goal here is to streamline the process, moving seamlessly from one dish to the next. For example, while your vegetables are roasting in the oven, you can have a pot of soup simmering on the stove and a batch of grains cooking in a rice cooker. This multitasking not only saves time but also makes the most of your kitchen resources.

Portioning is another critical aspect of batch cooking. Once your dishes are cooked, divide them into individual servings. This step is crucial for staying on track with your dietary goals. Proper portion control ensures that you're consuming the right number of calories and nutrients at each meal. Invest in a good set of containers that are both microwave-safe and freezer-friendly. Label each container with the date and contents to make meal selection easy throughout the week.

One of the significant advantages of batch cooking is its flexibility. You can customize meals to suit your preferences and dietary needs. If you're following Dr. Nowzaradan's plan, focus on creating dishes that are low in calories but high in nutrients. Incorporate plenty of lean proteins, vegetables, and whole grains to keep your meals balanced and satisfying. Additionally, you can easily adjust the seasonings and flavors to prevent meal fatigue, ensuring that your meals remain enjoyable day after day.

Finally, batch cooking is not just about convenience; it's about consistency. By committing to this practice, you establish a routine that supports long-term success. You're less likely to stray from your dietary goals when healthy meals are readily available, and you reduce the temptation to indulge in less nutritious options. Over time, this consistency becomes a habit, making healthy eating a natural and effortless part of your lifestyle.

In essence, batch cooking is a powerful tool for anyone looking to maintain a healthy diet amidst a busy schedule. It allows you to take control of your meals, ensuring that you're always prepared with nutritious options, no matter what the week throws at you.

11.3 CREATING YOUR OWN MEAL PLANS

Designing your own meal plan is a deeply personal and empowering process. It's an opportunity to align your diet not just with your nutritional needs but also with your tastes, lifestyle, and goals. While following a structured plan can be effective, customizing your meals allows for flexibility, sustainability, and, importantly, enjoyment in your journey towards better health.

The first step in creating your meal plan is understanding your unique nutritional needs. This is where you define your goals—whether they involve weight loss, muscle gain, or simply maintaining a healthy balance. Understanding these goals will help you determine the right macronutrient ratios for your meals. For instance, if you're following Dr. Nowzaradan's plan, the focus will be on reducing calorie intake while maximizing nutrition through lean proteins, fiber-rich vegetables, and whole grains.

Once you have a clear sense of your nutritional requirements, consider your daily schedule. Are you someone who thrives on routine, or do you need more flexibility? If you have a busy lifestyle, simplicity and ease of preparation might be key factors. In contrast, if you enjoy cooking, you might want to experiment with more elaborate recipes. The key is to create a plan that fits seamlessly into your life rather than one that feels like an additional chore.

Next, think about variety. While it's important to have staples that you can rely on—like grilled chicken, steamed vegetables, or a favorite breakfast smoothie—variety is what keeps a meal plan interesting and sustainable. Explore different cuisines, experiment with new ingredients, and don't be afraid to adapt recipes to suit your tastes. For example, if you find a particular vegetable unappealing, swap it out for one you enjoy. The goal is to make your meal plan something you look forward to, rather than a monotonous obligation.

When it comes to portion control, it's crucial to find a balance that satisfies your hunger while aligning with your health goals. This may involve some trial and error. Start by following general portion guidelines, but listen to your body—adjustments might be necessary depending on how you feel after meals. Over time, you'll develop a keen sense of what portions work best for you, ensuring you stay nourished and energized throughout the day.

Incorporating flexibility into your meal plan is also essential. Life is unpredictable, and strict adherence to a rigid plan can sometimes lead to frustration. Build in options for days when things don't go as planned—perhaps a few quick, healthy meals that can be thrown together in minutes, or the occasional indulgence that won't derail your progress. Flexibility is what makes a meal plan sustainable in the long run.

Finally, remember that a meal plan is not set in stone. It should evolve as you do—adapting to your changing tastes, goals, and lifestyle. Regularly review your plan, reflect on what's working and what's not, and be open to making changes. The process of creating and adjusting your meal plan is ongoing, and with each adjustment, you're honing a tool that supports your health and well-being in the best possible way.

By taking the time to create a meal plan tailored to your needs, preferences, and lifestyle, you're setting yourself up for long-term success. This personalized approach not only makes healthy eating more enjoyable but also more effective, ensuring that your diet becomes a natural and fulfilling part of your everyday life.

A NOTE OF GRATITUDE

Dear Reader,

Thank you for purchasing my book! I hope you find the same joy in reading it as I did in writing it. Your support means a lot to me.

I would appreciate it if you could spare a moment to leave a review! Your feedback helps me grow and aids other readers in their choices.

As a small gesture of thanks, please scan the QR code below to access your complimentary bonus content.

Thank you once again for your wonderful support!

Warm regards,

Darla Robson

[QR Code]

Made in United States
Orlando, FL
18 May 2025

61411526R00061